The BELIEVER'S ATMOSPHERE

DANIEL NYAH ALLO

The Believer's Atmosphere

Unless otherwise stated, Scripture quotations are taken from the **King James Version** of the Bible.

<u>Printed by:</u>
Universal Services Cameroon Sarl

Contact:

Daniel Nyah Allo

info@danielnyah.org

www.danielnyah.org

(+237) 654 512 218/243 858 491

By mastering your atmosphere, you easily influence your changes and experiences.

— Daniel Nyah Allo.

Contents

INTRODUCTION

You can Master Your changes

When you understand the delicate purpose of an atmosphere, you become the master of your changes. Nothing changes by chance. For every effect there is a cause, just as for every harvest there is a seed. One of the critical and fundamental requirements or advantages to effect changes in life is atmosphere. As important as seeds (or causes) are to creating a harvest (or change), they will amount to nothing without the wisdom of time, which waits for the right season in order to obtain the results. Waiting is wisdom. The purpose of the waiting period is to let the right season occur, and this can be told by the atmosphere.

In 2 Chronicles 12:32, the Bible tells us of the children of Issachar, saying,

"… which were men that had understanding of the times, to know what Israel ought to do; …"

Israel was certainly blessed to have had such men amongst them; they gave Israel the advantage of effecting right changes by having people able to tell them what they ought to do and at what time. These men understood the value of atmosphere to the point where they were described as men who had "…**understanding of the times**…" Knowing what to do and missing out on the timing can result in frustrations. The due time, which can be told by the atmosphere makes all things beautiful. It is said, God "…**hath made every thing beautiful in his time: …**" (Ecclesiastes 3:11). God Himself has restricted beauty to the right time. The time cannot be right and the atmosphere wrong; no. When the time is right, then the atmosphere has equally been set right.

Atmosphere decides what flourishes and what dies; it decides what is attracted and what is resisted. Atmospheres decide the restfulness and excellence of a man's pursuits.

Sometimes, to change certain things, all we need to do is change the atmosphere. Paul and Silas didn't pray about the chains while in prison. They just changed the atmosphere and the chains lost their grip on them. My son sleeps better in a cold atmosphere. It takes a lot of effort for him to fall asleep when it is hot. Therefore, one of the best and easiest ways to make him sleep and sleep extensively, is to create the right atmosphere.

Understanding atmospheres makes it easy for us to rightly expect and create our desired changes. Everything is programmed to be beautiful only in its time. In this book —*The Believer's Atmosphere*, you will find out how instrumental an atmosphere is to an expected change, why atmospheres exist, how to influence your atmosphere, and how to influence others in a positive way by your atmosphere. Something about you and around you is fundamentally deciding how things and people resonate towards you. Understanding the kind of atmosphere God wants you to carry at all times, will ensure that you maintain certain seasons in your life which are consistent with God's perfect will for you. A change of atmosphere can resolve a long-time difficulty or frustration, and cause progressive motion in the direction of your true purpose in God.

CHAPTER ONE

UNDERSTANDING ATMOSPHERES

Atmosphere and Changes

Not everything thrives in every place and at all times. This is a fact; it is how the earth, things, and man function. When the Lord God formed the earth, He said,

"… Let there be lights in the firmament of the heaven to divide the day from the night; and let them be for signs, and for seasons, and for days, and years:" (Genesis 1:14).

In other words, God programmed these lights to divide the day from the night (the rotation of the earth about the sun), they will provide signs, seasons, days, and years. *One of the greatest wisdoms a person can ever possess in life is that which demonstrates mastery of place, seasons, and atmospheres.* Things and people upon the earth are made or conditioned to succeed or fail based on how much they honour their place, seasons, and atmospheres.

After Noah and his family survived the flood, having offered an acceptable sacrifice unto the Lord, the Bible records that the Lord God responded to that by saying,

"While the earth remaineth, seedtime and harvest, and cold and heat, and summer and winter, and day and night shall not cease" (Genesis 8:22).

Once again, we can see the things that will remain on this earth for as long as the earth remains. In other words, there will always be a need to seed and to harvest; there will always be a cold season and a hot season; there will always be summer and winter. The cycle of day and night shall not cease. If a man's harvest determines the quality of his life, then understanding seasons and the ability to influence them is fundamental to a truly productive life. Wisdom says:

"Whoso keepeth the commandment shall feel no evil thing: and <u>a wise man's heart discerneth both time and judgment</u>" (Ecclesiastes 8:5).

A man's ability to tell a season is key to knowing what atmosphere to expect, just as the ability to tell the atmosphere points to what season is active. The verse we read says if you are wise, then your heart is able to tell both the time and the judgment (action). Things do not just happen at any time, be it your body, relationships, academics, or business, etc. Attempting the right thing at the wrong time will result in frustration. Atmospheres reveal the readiness of a place.

If you know a thing's place (or atmosphere), you can influence the atmosphere to either resist it or attract it.

Man has the ability to create the change required for a desired experienced. He can do this by making the atmosphere consistent with that which is desired, or inconsistent with that which is not. A man's atmosphere will decide what is promoted or resisted; it will decide what comes or what leaves; what flourishes or what dies. Something a man does not have may be revealing an atmosphere he has not created, just as something that comes towards a man may be responding to a friendly atmosphere.

The Lord Jesus Christ said,

"For wheresoever the carcase is, there will the eagles be gathered together" (Matthew 24:28).

What is it that attracts the eagles? It is not just the carcase but the quality of the atmosphere influenced by the smell from the carcase. In other words, atmospheres attract or repel. *That is a law being revealed there; that something you need waits for an atmosphere, meanwhile something you may have (which you do not like) is staying because there is a conducive atmosphere.* It is said,

"A soft answer turneth away wrath: but grievous words stir up anger" (Proverbs 15:1).

In other words, wrath does not do well in a "soft atmosphere"; a soft atmosphere suffocates wrath. So, instead of making wrath your focus, make the atmosphere your focus and it will effortlessly turn away wrath. This is too important, especially for different types of relationships; atmospheres are critical to what becomes of our experiences in life.

Ants do not follow sugar because they see it. Rather, they smell the fragrance being released by the sugar (which changes the atmosphere) and are drawn to it. What is an atmosphere?

In meteorological terms, an atmosphere is the weather or climate surrounding a given place, which can be perceived by the temperature, the cloud, or the wind.

Anywhere in the world is "a place". In fact, wherever you are is a place. Not only do people inhabit places in the world, but people are "places" as well. The "weather or climate" in that place decides what happens there. Wisdom demands that we focus primarily on our atmosphere and not necessarily on "the need" or desired change. *Wanting or desiring something does not necessarily mean you are going to get it, unless you create a friendly atmosphere for it.* Something a man does not want is not leaving because there is a friendly atmosphere which promotes its presence. When Paul and Silas were locked up in prison, it was a change in atmosphere that brought forth their miracle. Instead of focusing on the chains, they rather focused on the atmosphere. How did they do that? The Bible says,

"And at midnight PAUL AND SILAS PRAYED, AND SANG PRAISES UNTO GOD: and the prisoners heard them. And suddenly there was a great earthquake, so that the foundations of the prison were shaken: and immediately all the doors were opened, and every one's bands were loosed" (Acts 16:25/26).

Do you think things would have been any different without the prayers and praises? Certainly not. *When things change, things change.* Their prayers and praises changed their atmosphere and made for the experience of their liberty from the chains. In other words, the atmosphere they created was not consistent with captivity. Consequently, captivity gave way to freedom. It is said, *"…suddenly there was a great earthquake, …and immediately all the doors were opened, and every one's bands were loosed."* It is a clear illustration of the changes which take place when a people's atmosphere changes. Unfortunately, when the Lord's people were asked to praise God while in captivity, they rather became so overwhelmed by their captivity and replied,

"How shall we sing the LORD'S song in a strange land?" (Psalms 137:4).

Well, had they understood the wisdom behind the instruction—*the atmosphere of liberty it was meant to create*, they would have rather than giving a reason not. Paul and Silas got this working in their favour by praying and praising God, despite their unfavourable condition. That is why it is important to trust in the Lord with all our hearts, and not lean on our own understanding. Waiting for convenient circumstances in order to do God's Word may keep a man in discomfort too long.

The Purpose of an Atmosphere

An atmosphere exists to decide what changes can occur at a given place. Atmospheres fundamentally decide purpose consistency. Everything looks for its atmosphere of comfort and flees from an atmosphere of discomfort; it will neither show up nor stay until the atmosphere is convenient. The Bible says,

"If the clouds be full of rain, they empty themselves upon the earth: ..." (Ecclesiastes 11:3).

Rain falls when the clouds are full. In the sections ahead, we will see how even the clouds decide the atmosphere. *In other words, if you can fill the cloud, you can change the atmosphere and decide rain fall.* At a given time, this was impossible, but it is now made possible via Cloud Seeding Technology. The following article (available on the internet) shows how this works:

Dubai and other emirates in the United Arab Emirates are creating rain through cloud seeding technology, hoping to bring year-around precipitation to the sun-baked land.

I've been to Dubai several times over the years during the summer months. The weather is always the same: extremely hot, often with only scattered clouds in the sky. During my recent visit, a hot morning suddenly turned into a stormy afternoon and evening. I was on a boat and as the clouds rolled in, thunder emanated from them. When I commented on it, my host said: "Oh yeah, they're manipulating the weather here. They seed the clouds." Apparently, this is not new technology nor exclusive to Dubai. The UAE has been experimenting in weather manipulation for two decades. But I certainly saw it on display for the first time…and loved it. According to the Khaleej Times: Although cloud seeding, which the UAE adopted in the early 1990s, is not an exact science, the process of shooting salt flares into the clouds has increased the chance of rain in the country by 15-25 per cent. Since January, the National Centre of Meteorology has conducted over 100 missions and the results have been fruitful: more rain has fallen. The UAE averages only about 100mm of water per year.

Khalid Mohamed Al Obeidli, head of cloud seeding at the National Centre of Meteorology, added: More rainfall will help ease the water stress, and cloud seeding is cheaper (costs around 1 fil per cubic metre of water produced as compared to 60 fils needed to desalinate the same amount of water) and more environment-friendly than desalination. Scientists cannot create clouds, only manipulate clouds to become storm clouds. Seeding will continue this summer.

Dubai is actually a destination I like to avoid this time of year due to the intense heat. That said, if cloud seeding brings rains (without intense humidity) and more temperate weather, I think Dubai and other emirates would draw a lot more tourists during the summer months.

Isn't it amazing what humans can do about their atmospheres? You see, one of the great advantages of wisdom is the ability to invent solutions or chart a way where there is no way. Wisdom speaking says,

"I wisdom dwell with prudence, and find out knowledge of witty inventions" (Proverbs 8:12).

There are people in our world today who do not know that there is such a thing as Cloud Seeding Technology. Consequently, instead of mastering their changes by influencing their atmospheres, they are at the mercy of any change. Dubai "manipulates" its weather to provoke rain. In Chapter Five, we are going to see how, as believers, we can influence our atmospheres for the best of God's will to be revealed. The conclusion of that article says, Dubai and the Emirates will draw a lot more tourists during summer because cloud seeding brings more rain, resulting in a more temperate and conducive atmosphere for tourists.

A man who is able to master his atmosphere is able to intentionally influence his changes. Everyone at any given time has an atmosphere. You just have to find out which one you carry every day.

1) Atmosphere Decides Presence

Not everyone can stand every atmosphere. Certain persons will either be comfortable or uncomfortable around a given atmosphere. As an aroma draws or repels certain things, so are atmospheres with people. If you know who you want and know what they like, it is easy to intentionally create an atmosphere consistent with who they are. The choice or kind of people who come or leave is basically atmosphere dependent. We can make our lives comfortable for the Spirit of the Lord and for angels, or we can make our lives consistent with the presence of demons or evil things. *If God inhabits the praises of Israel, then atmosphere decides presence.*

When the Lord Jesus Christ sent the disciples to go preach the gospel of the Kingdom, He said to them,

"And into whatsoever house ye enter, first say, Peace be to this house. And if the son of peace be there, your peace shall rest upon it: if not, it shall turn to you again" (Luke 10:5/6).

We all, consciously or unconsciously resonate towards where we are accepted and where our values are promoted. There will be no peace in the absence of the son of peace. Therefore, there is a certain atmosphere which is consistent with peace, for peace to stay or abide. The atmosphere there decides presence. If there be a son of peace in the house, then peace will abide for as long as he allows the atmosphere to be consistent with the guest of peace.

2) Atmosphere Decides Changes

As earlier seen, one of the best ways to change things is to change the atmosphere. There are things which suffocate in a given environment while others thrive in the same. One of the best ways to heal your body is to make your body uncomfortable for the disease. Though there are diverse scientific ways of doing this, we will look at the spiritual way, which goes beyond the limits of science. Atmosphere can decide a change in a conversation and even the subject. There are certain people whose facial expression do not permit a certain subject; by just changing the looks on their faces, they immediately change the atmosphere and change the conversation.

Wisdom says,

"The north wind driveth away rain: so doth an angry countenance a backbiting tongue" (Proverbs 25:23).

Most people who listen to gossip entertain it by their appearance. There is a look which says, "Tell me more"; it creates an atmosphere consistent with the conversation. The verse we just read says there is a look which drives away a backbiter as the north wind drives away the rain. Atmosphere decides changes. Every change is looking for a friendly atmosphere; when it finds it, it gets in and stays. *Do not drive the flies; stop the stench. Do not drive the ants; remove the sugar. Do not stop the vultures; take away the carcase.*

3) Atmosphere Decides Happenings

Everything is beautiful in its time. A lot of the good things God desires for His children will be suspended until they create the right atmosphere. That you desire a thing, does not necessarily imply that you are ready for it. Desire alone is not enough proof of readiness; atmosphere is. The liberty Paul and Silas had to experience was waiting for a change in atmosphere. The goodwill of God is at liberty to manifest when the atmosphere is consistent with God's desire for His children.

The Evil of Manipulation

You can always manipulate an atmosphere to your own detriment. It is deception when a manipulated atmosphere presents itself as ready, when in actual fact it is not. Such deceptions are the fruits of haste. Wisdom says,

"A faithful man shall abound with blessings: but he that maketh haste to be rich shall not be innocent" (Proverbs 28:20).

In other words, that which alters the standard will end up making man a victim. There are many ways in life crafted by men, by which they bypass the due process to an end. And the end they meet is not as sweet as they expected it to be. As said, God has only made beauty for its time. Arriving God's time requires the process of diligence and submission to due process. This is what makes for the faithfulness of a man, resulting in him being blessed indeed, without sorrow.

It is written,

"The blessing of the LORD, it maketh rich, and he addeth no sorrow with it" (Proverbs 10:22).

It is not God's blessing until it is God's time. And it is not God's time until it is God's way. So, what we call the blessing of God indeed is "the way" of God; it does not lead to destruction but to life. This can only be experienced by faithful men. Faithful speaks of a patient and diligent adherence to the ways of God. This causes a man to allow himself and things to develop according to God's purpose, until the time for the beauty of God to be revealed. When this happens, then the atmosphere is made consistent with God's most excellent purpose. So, it is said, **"A faithful man shall abound with blessings: but he that maketh haste to be rich**

shall not be innocent" (Proverbs 28:20). The hasty man shall not be innocent because he will be guilty of the breach of protocol and procedure. Hence, he will not be ready for that which is expected. In other words, he will not be innocent of the sorrow that will befall him.

It is good wisdom not to manipulate an atmosphere so that it appears consistent with what is expected, when indeed it is not ready for it. Truth makes free; it blesses indeed and makes rich. When we allow or subject things to due process, we end up enjoying the fruit of glory. Here is where this caution is vital;

"There is a way which seemeth right unto a man, but the end thereof are the ways of death" (Proverbs 14:12).

The end of any form of manipulation is death, no matter how beautiful it may seem to appear at the beginning.

Atmosphere and Influence

At any given time, you are either influencing others by your atmosphere or being influenced by the atmospheres of others. On a daily basis, at any given moment, we are either sharing our atmosphere with others or sharing the atmospheres of others. The question then is; what is your atmosphere providing? Your atmosphere is either bringing a blessing into the lives of others or a curse; you are either helping others excel or keeping them stagnant by the atmosphere you bring or create. Our atmospheres do not just end with us. Those within the diameter of our atmosphere can have the same experience as us. This can be a huge advantage, depending on what kind of atmosphere is created or exists. That is why it is said,

"He that walketh with wise men shall be wise: but a companion of fools shall be destroyed" (Proverbs 13:20).

The main reason for becoming wise when walking with the wise is because you share in the blessing of their atmosphere, for every atmosphere has what it promotes or resists by the fragrance it carries or emanates. *Wisdom is the fragrance in the atmosphere of the wise. Anyone within that atmosphere shares the same.* Therefore, the atmosphere that unfriendly atmosphere to destruction; destruction does not thrive in such atmospheres. On the other hand, the one within the company (atmosphere) of fools shall be destroyed. In other words, the atmosphere of fools attracts destruction; it is a friendly atmosphere to the things that destroy. That is why it is so important to mind your company; for it decides your changes. Mind the atmosphere you carry, for it is also deciding the changes in others.

There are some people whose lives changed for better or for worst ever since they started a certain relationship or joined a certain company. What fundamentally changed? Atmosphere. The atmosphere began influencing them positively or negatively. And since two are better than one because they have a good reward for their labour, things become better or worse, if those in the relationship are committed to the same atmosphere. So, what used to happen once in their lives may begin happening a thousand times more; the presence, the changes, and happenings now have a multiplier effect. That is the power behind atmosphere and influence.

Some relationships or companies have atmospheres which are consistent with good experiences, while others have atmospheres which promote evil. Atmospheres decide motivation. You either override a given atmosphere in your favour, or quit or flee the current atmosphere. There are certain things we have the power to change and others we only have the power to flee. It is wisdom to know when to preserve your current atmosphere by fleeing a given atmosphere.

The Bible says,

"Flee fornication. Every sin that a man doeth is without the body; but he that committeth fornication sinneth against his own body" (1 Corinthians 6:18).

In other words, the atmosphere of fornication is not one you can override or superimpose on; so, do not fight it; flee from it. Do not pray about it, flee. Such an atmosphere can only attract destruction. On the other hand, God's Word tells us,

"Submit yourselves therefore to God. Resist the devil, and he will flee from you" (James 4:7).

In this case, we are not to flee from the devil but resist him and make him flee; we are to maintain our atmosphere until he can no longer stand it. There are atmospheres which can suffocate the devil. We will see how to do this in Chapter Five: The Believer's Atmosphere. Our atmosphere can be shared; it can equally be extended to others and influence what becomes of their experiences. Whenever an atmosphere changes—*just like with season*—it is a sign that a certain change is about to take place. *To master your atmosphere is to be a blessing to others.* This is one of the ways we share God's goodness in our lives with others.

For example, in the case we saw earlier about Paul and Silas—*who prayed and sang praises to God though being in prison*; they triggered a change of atmosphere which did not just bless them but equally blessed the other prisoners. It is said, when they prayed and sang praises, "...**the prisoners heard them**..." As they did, there was an extension of the atmosphere to them, and they too experienced the change—*liberty*—which was attracted into that atmosphere. It is said, "....**and immediately all the doors were opened, and EVERY ONE'S BANDS WERE LOOSED**" (Acts 16:26).

You see, the doors did not open just for Paul and Silas; no, they opened for all in the prison too. The chains did not just fall off from Paul and Silas. It is said, "...everyone's bands were loosed."

Isn't it amazing what influence a certain atmosphere can have on others? Think of what carrying this kind of an atmosphere will do in the life of your family members, friends, colleagues, or even strangers.

Made for Influence

Humans are made for influence; their lives are to have a positive effect on others; they are made in God's image to share His goodness in their lives with others. So, from the beginning of creation, we see the almighty God assign the role of influence to man when He said,

"… **Let us make man in our image, after our likeness: and let them have dominion over the fish of the sea, and over the fowl of the air, and over the cattle, and over all the earth, and over every creeping thing that creepeth upon the earth**" (Genesis 1:26).

"To have dominion" is to be given the authority to decide the course of affairs over the earth. Man was responsible for giving direction to creation, and deciding the outcome of circumstances. This responsibility of influence was not given to man only for creation, it was also given to Cain and Abel to be used towards each other. When God reprimanded Cain for not dealing wisely with his responsibilities, he became angry and acted otherwise; he abused the purpose of his influence and went ahead to kill his brother.

The responsibility to influence positively was illustrated when God came to Cain and asked,

"… Cain, Where is Abel thy brother? …"

And Cain replied, **"… Am I my brother's keeper?"** (Genesis 4:9).

What a response! He was in direct rebellion to his responsibility to have a blessed influence over his brother by letting his brother share in the blessedness of his atmosphere. Rather, he created an atmosphere of hate and nurtured it until it became convenient enough for sin. Prior to Cain developing a bad atmosphere of influence, the Lord had told him this:

"If thou doest well, shalt thou not be accepted? and if thou doest not well, sin lieth at the door. And unto thee shall be his desire, and thou shalt rule over him" (Genesis 4:7).

Sin was only at the door because of the atmosphere Cain created in the house. "Sin lieth at the door" speaks of how close sin was to ruling over him. Instead of sin ruling over Cain, God expected him to rule over sin by embracing the right atmosphere of influence (that is the atmosphere of love). An atmosphere his brother Abel could have benefitted from. Man is made to be a "keeper of his brother" by building an atmosphere profitable to his brother. Man is made for influence. So, it is said,

"Neither do men light a candle, and put it under a bushel, but on a candlestick; and it giveth light unto all that are in the house" (Matthew 5:15).

In other words, after being lit, you also need a strategic position, if your light is going to be a blessing beyond yourself. That's called influence—*when your life is able to cause changes in others*. This is the reason why it is so important to mind what effect your atmosphere is having on others. Because we are made for *positive influence*; we are to cause things – *whether in our lives or in that of others* – to go the way of the Lord; the way of righteousness. That is the believers' call.

The verse we read above says, **"…it gives light unto all that are in the house…"** This expressly speaks of influence. That is the purpose of a person's atmosphere, based on what it offers, be it something good or something bad. The Bible tells us,

"Have respect unto the covenant: for the dark places of the earth are full of the habitations of cruelty" (Psalms 74:20).

If the dark places of the earth are full of cruelty, then it means cruelty will cease to exist at the appearance of light. So, there is an atmosphere—*darkness*, which is consistent with cruelty. In other words, cruelty is attracted to dark places. So then, John says,

"And the light shineth in darkness; and the darkness comprehended it not" (John 1:5).

Light therefore makes for an atmosphere which is not friendly with darkness. This illustrates the vitality of an atmosphere and its relationship with influence. If our light shines across to others, then we get to help others experience freedom from cruelty which is friendly with dark places. Therefore, a person with a lighted atmosphere is a threat to the even to the darkness in the lives of others. Isn't this wonderful? For influence sake, no one lights a candle and puts it under a bushel but on a candlestick.

It is in this regard that the Lord Jesus Christ said,

"Let your light so shine before men, that they may see your good works, and glorify your Father which is in heaven" (Matthew 5:16).

Influence is when your light has an effect on something or someone else, and is causing movement in a direction dictated by your atmosphere. In the verse above, we are expected to influence others by making our light seen. In other words, people will be able to perceive the beauty of your atmosphere based on your activity in the light and realize that, this must be the workings of a good God. That is because humans are custodians of God's glory, having been made in His image. So, we are made for influence; you are made for influence. If you master your atmosphere, you will be directly or indirectly influencing the lives of those who walk into the diameter of your atmosphere or who are already within your sphere of contact.

We see the example of the Lord Jesus Christ, where there was this child tormented by evil spirits. As soon as the Lord Jesus Christ arrived the scene, it is said,

"...when he saw him, straightway the spirit tare him; and he fell on the ground, and wallowed foaming" (Mark 9:20).

This is remarkable because He had not said a word! Why did the evil spirit not go into operation when the disciples where there? Why did the spirit not wait for Him to talk? The difference was in the atmosphere He carried. The energy and intention of love in the atmosphere of Christ was different from that in His disciples and others who were present. The atmosphere the Lord Jesus Christ came with was already charged with faith and authority; it was so lighted that the evil spirit could not stand it. That is influence—*the ability to cause things and people to change their course or direction.* Imagine what would happen to people when God's children carry such an atmosphere at all times. They will be in effortless control of what comes and what leaves; they will be able to call forth that which is good and send off that which is bad, by the atmosphere they have embraced or created.

Leadership and Influence

Wisdom says,

"When the righteous are in authority, the people rejoice: but when the wicked beareth rule, the people mourn" (Proverbs 29:2).

Leadership is a position of responsibility for mass influence. Everyone under a leader is very likely to partake in the leader's atmosphere. That is why it is said, *"…when the righteous are in authority, the people rejoice."* On the contrary, *"…when the wicked beareth rule, the people mourn."* Did you see that leadership fundamentally decides what becomes of the state of a people? Whether a people mourn or rejoice, is highly dependent on leadership. The reason it happens so is because the atmosphere created by one man influences all those under his authority; that is what it means to lead.

Being in leadership is a very critical thing. And until those in authority understand how delicate their actions and atmospheres are to those they lead, change may never be intentional. *Leadership is God's wisdom not just for structure, but for the blessedness of many.* God's wisdom uses one or few to transform many. That has always been God's effortless way of bringing change to a people, be it a family, community, city, or nation. This is the reason why God values leadership; be it personal leadership, family leadership, community leadership, professional leadership, or governmental leadership. God is interested in the leader. *Leadership decides what becomes of a people's atmosphere.* The power to change an atmosphere over a given relationship or environment is in the hands of the leader; what leaves and what comes, what starts and what stops, is basically leadership dependent.

You are a leader over your body; the members of your body thrive or fail based on the quality of your leadership. They are dependent on the atmosphere you create for them by the food you eat, the thoughts you hold, or your activities. The responsibility to influence the atmosphere is in your hands. *Remember, leadership is the position for mass influence. It is an elevation for reference.* A leader is lifted for others to look up to; he inspires direction and action in people, thereby influencing what becomes of their atmosphere. John Maxwell says, "…*everything rises and falls on leadership*…"

A leader who is conscious of the responsibility and the power of influence can change an atmosphere for the well-being of a people. Esther was a leader who never understood the amount of power and responsibility in her position or office. While Haman planned to destroy the Jews, she did not understand she could influence that atmosphere, and resist such evil from coming to her people. But blessed be God for a good mentor like Mordecai (her foster father), who awakened Esther to the power in her leadership; he made Esther understand that she was able to influence the atmosphere set by Haman to bring death upon the Jews. She created an atmosphere which permitted the people to live and not die:

"Then Mordecai commanded to answer Esther, Think not with thyself that thou shalt escape in the king's house, more than all the Jews. For if thou altogether holdest thy peace at this time, then shall there enlargement and deliverance arise to the Jews from another place; but thou and thy father's house shall be destroyed: and who knoweth whether thou art come to the kingdom for such a time as this?" (Esther 4:13/14).

Esther was in the position to change the verdict which was passed over the Jews. That is the purpose of leadership. Thanks to the awakening brought by Mordecai, she stepped into her office, maximized the powers of her leadership position, and saved the Jews from being destroyed by their enemies. The Jews were about to suffer death and mourning by the hands of a Haman (a wicked ruler); but Esther (the righteous ruler) overturned it and rather made the people to rejoice. The power to change the atmosphere and resist death, was in her hands and she used it wisely. Halleluiah.

At the least, everyone is a leader of his or her body; you can decide how well your body flourishes. You can decide what direction it goes and what experiences it gets. You can do this by taking up quality leadership over your body and deciding what it attracts or repels by the atmospheres you create. For example, James says,

"For in many things we offend all. If any man offend not in word, the same is a perfect man, and able also to bridle the whole body. Behold, we put bits in the horses' mouths, that

they may obey us; and we turn about their whole body. Behold also the ships, which though they be so great, and are driven of fierce winds, yet are they turned about with a very small helm, whithersoever the governor listeth. Even so the tongue is a little member, and boasteth great things. Behold, how great a matter a little fire kindleth!" (James 3:2-5).

That speaks of the power and beauty of leadership. As heavy as your body and destiny are, your choice of words can decide their direction and experiences. That is what James is saying; that is leadership and influence at work. Mastering the wisdom of atmospheres will fundamentally decide your changes. Remember, what comes or what leaves is atmosphere dependent.

CHAPTER TWO

ATMOSPHERE AND THE LAW OF FAVOUR

You can Influence Favour

The law of favour, known to science as the law of attraction is real. Everything is attracted to its type or to that which gives it pleasure. *If you want to attract something, be what the thing is interested in or is compatible with.* This law, as we have seen in Chapter One, governs everything about life; from humans, to animals, and insects. Everything resonates towards its interest. The Lord Jesus Christ, who is the wisdom of God, said,

"For wheresoever the carcase is, there will the eagles be gathered together" (Matthew 24:28).

Who or what a man is, is deciding or influencing what he is attracting or attracted to. Who you are influences how people and things respond towards you and how you respond towards things and people. Something about your atmosphere is basically deciding reactions towards you. That is why the Lord Jesus Christ revealing how true this is, said, "…**wheresoever the carcase is, there will the eagles be gathered together.**" This simply means that if you want the gathering of eagles (or want to attract eagles), be or have the carcase. As seen earlier, the eagles are not primary attracted by what they see, but by what they smell. *The smell from the carcase is what forms the atmosphere that attracts the eagles.* Eagles respond favourably to their interest; they are attracted by that which has what they desire.

It goes the same for other very natural things we see in life daily. Monkeys are attracted to bananas, ants are attracted to sugar, and even mosquitoes are known to be attracted to type O blood-group persons. It is not the sight of the things they like, but the savour or fragrance those things emit. When you see your favourite fruit, what first attracts you to it is not the sight but the savour which is already within you. The sight of it only triggers the savour or atmosphere expected around it, because it is already in you. *What is in us is the reason for our external attractions.* We will not be attracted to something unless it first exists within us. The Bible tells us,

"Be sober, be vigilant; because your adversary the devil, as a roaring lion, <u>walketh about, seeking whom he may devour</u>:" (1 Peter 5:8).

Who does the devil find good enough to devour? Those with his kind of atmosphere; they possess that which is the devil's. What is within a man creates an atmosphere around him which makes him either a prey or victor. So, the Lord Jesus Christ said,

"Hereafter I will not talk much with you: for the prince of this world cometh, <u>and hath nothing in me</u>" (John 14:30).

In other words, the Lord Jesus was saying, "*I do not have his property in me. Hence, I do not have an atmosphere consistent with his desires; he can neither stay around nor devour me.*" So, the prince of this world (Satan) could not devour the Lord Jesus Christ because he had nothing in Him. Isn't that wonderful? The Lord Jesus Christ understood this law of favour (or attraction); He knew how to put it to work to His advantage.

Nothing attracts a person externally unless it is first found within the person. What makes for our attractions are the similarities between what is internal and what is external. That is why James says,

"But every man is tempted, when he is drawn away of his own lust, and enticed" (James 1:14).

In other words, temptation will not exist unless it first finds lust in a man. An atmosphere is like the fruit that makes us recognize a tree. The atmosphere that attracts you, primarily reveals what is within you.

It is without doubt, that you are attracted to something someone is or has. Likewise, someone is attracted to a quality of yours or something that you have. *That therefore means, if you can influence who you are, you can decide who and what you attract, and who you are attracted to.* It is for this reason the Bible says,

"… **For where your treasure is, there will your heart be also**" (Luke 12:34).

That is a principle. Every heart is drawn towards its interest or treasure. *If you have what men need or desire, men will respond toward you in a gracious manner. God has made men and the universe in such a way that everything gravitates towards its interest or pleasure. Every man or thing invests the most where he is pleasured the most. If you become a man's pleasure, you become his attraction. Just as when you become what a man detests, you become what he shuns.*

When you become a point of interest, and attract the graciousness of an interested person, then you have been favoured. You cannot be a swine and expect to deserve a precious pearl. A gold ring is not for a pig's nose. If you want any man to delight in you, then be, have, or do what is of interest to him. That is a universal principle which sets the law of favour in motion for all men.

The Bible speaking of the prophet Samuel says,

"And the child Samuel grew on, and was in favour both with the LORD, and also with men" (1 Samuel 2:26).

This was not said of Samuel alone, but also of our Lord Jesus Christ:

"And Jesus increased in wisdom and stature, and in favour with God and man" (Luke 2:52).

Neither Samuel nor Jesus Christ experience this favour by chance; no. It was not a gift. They knew what to do to gain the favour of God and man. Favour is the result of a man's attractiveness. *The more delightful you become, the more favour you attract.* Favour is the result of having a good understanding of life and living in a manner consistent with the delights of life and people. This lifestyle creates an atmosphere, which attracts the kindness or graciousness of both God and man towards a person. Wisdom says,

"Let not mercy and truth forsake thee: bind them about thy neck; write them upon the table of thine heart: So shalt thou

find favour and good understanding in the sight of God and man" (Proverbs 3:3/4).

You see, where there is mercy and truth bound around a person's neck, then favour and good understanding in the sight of God and man will become his experience. Think about that. You can intentionally influence the favour you experience in life; it is neither a gift nor a thing of chance.

Becoming a Person of Favour

Any man can attract the extraordinary by being what the extraordinary is attracted to. A wise person knows how to get the king's attention by being who or what the king is pleasured by or attracted to. Dr Mike Murdock says, "There is a king in every environment." *There is something you have to be in order to attract what you desire.* And what you desire has to find what it desires in you in order to stay. You do not need some special advice to choose where your joy comes from over where your pain or sorrow comes from. Does a man need advice to choose joy over sorrow? So it is said,

"Thou wilt shew me the path of life: <u>in thy presence is fulness of joy</u>; at thy right hand there are pleasures for evermore"

(Psalms 16:11).

Every human is inwardly searching for life—*for joy and pleasures.* Except a being is corrupted, there is no one at peace with pain and sorrow. There is no way we can be attracted to God except there is the guarantee or assurance of joy and pleasures. The verse above tells us that is who God is and what He has. So, there is something about God's atmosphere (which comes from who He is), that satisfies that which a man is truly in search of—*life.* Every man from within longs to live. So, whenever God is revealed, it is impossible for a man not to be attracted to Him, because within a man is the craving for life. God knows what to be to attract man to Himself. In His presence is fullness of joy and at His right hand there are pleasures forevermore. Amen.

Be intentional about attracting what you want and repelling what you do not want. You can do a self-check to verify what is making something or someone not come to you or not to stay around you. There are people to whom riches are attracted because they have what riches like. On the other hand, riches flee from some, because they have the wrong atmosphere. *Self-sanctification means separating yourself from that which attracts what you really do not want or need.* That in itself is great wisdom. Favour is no mystery; it follows what it likes. Paul the apostle said,

"…**If a man therefore <u>purge himself from these</u>, he shall be a vessel unto honour, sanctified, and meet for the master's use, and prepared unto every good work**" (2 Timothy 2:21).

That is very enlightening. To be a vessel of interest or pleasure to the master, there is need for purging; there is a need to cut off from the things which do not please the Master. This makes a person an honourable vessel for the Master's delightful use. In other words, you will gain the master's favour.

As a jewel of gold in a swine's snout, so is a fair woman which is without discretion (Proverbs 11:22).

In other words, a poor character discredits a woman's beauty. Wisdom compares such to a jewel of gold in swine's snout. That is a lot to learn. So, the Lord Jesus Christ cautions along this line saying,

"Give not that which is holy unto the dogs, neither cast ye your pearls before swine, lest they trample them under their feet, and turn again and rend you" (Matthew 7:6).

There is always a state or behaviour that decides a man's favour; holy things are not for dogs and pearls are not for swine. The Bible tells us of the extraordinary ascend of Esther to becoming queen.

Though her favour was extraordinary, it was not without extraordinary measures. It had a cost as most valuable things would demand. She maximized the law of favour. Before qualifying for favour, Esther and the other virgins were set apart for twelve months of purification or "purging" (Esther 2:12). It is said, they were given

"…six months with oil of myrrh, and six months with sweet odours, and with other things for the purifying of the women; …"

This procedure was necessary to make them fit enough to be what the king delights or takes pleasure in; they had to match the standard or become consistent with that which pleased the king. By this sanctification process, something the king did not like had to leave them, for something the king liked to come in. Favour is not blind; it does not without preparation, perception, and personal preferences. *Favour is not without being something or someone of interest;* it is responding graciously towards something or someone. Favour has a cause and a cost.

Favour is the gracious response of a person or thing towards another by taking delight in who the person is or in what the person has.

So, the Psalmist tells us,

"Thou shalt arise, and have mercy upon Zion: for the time to favour her, yea, the set time, is come" (Psalms 102:13).

The time of Zion's favour did not come without an activity pleasing to God. The reason given for Zion's set time of favour (which caused Zion experience mercy) was,

"For thy servants take pleasure in her stones, and favour the dust thereof" (Psalms 102:14).

The reason God's favour came upon the people of Zion, is because they took pleasure in the stones of Zion and showed interests in the durst thereof. They became (by their interest) what God delights in.

Who a person is or what a person has that attracts the attention and kindness of another, is called *the flavour of favour; that flavour is what changes a person's atmosphere.* That is what Esther acquired during the twelve months of preparatory; she created the atmosphere for her favour before the king. It is said, when it was her turn to come before the king…

"…she required nothing but what Hegai the king's chamberlain, the keeper of the women, appointed. And Esther obtained favour in the sight of all them that looked

upon her" (Esther 2:15).

Maybe the king took delight in a simple woman, and not one all covered with jewels. Esther was prepared to attract the king's attention and to secure his favour. Something Esther required and received from the chamberlain is what distinguished her from the rest of the virgins; Esther looked like what the king and his men wanted; she had the expected flavour and carried the desired atmosphere for the king's liking. In other words, she had the atmosphere that triggered that which was in the king, and influenced his reaction. Esther's chamberlain knew how to create the right atmosphere for to gain the king's favour. Such people in your life are golden; people who teach you how to detox yourself in order to become a vessel of honour. That helps you to attract that which is right for your life according to God's perfect will. Do you have such people in your life? That was Esther's mentor; and that is what mentorship is for. It is written:

"And the king loved Esther above all the women, and she obtained grace and favour in his sight more than all the virgins; so that he set the royal crown upon her head, and made her queen instead of Vashti" (Esther 2:17).

To love Esther means he derived more pleasure in looking at Esther than the other women; he was attracted to who Esther was, what she had on, how she smelled, and how she talked. *To attract, you have to be it.* This was the case with Joseph and Daniel. Something someone is seeing in or with you is deciding his or her reaction towards you. Something you are or have is deciding the atmosphere and attention around you. It is an undeniable fact which God Himself responds to.

A man's gift maketh room for him, and bringeth him before great men (Proverbs 18:16).

The difference in men is the pleasure they provide for people and to things; the difference in men is their atmosphere, which decides their favour. Your atmosphere will decide what comes and what leaves. That is why it is important to retain these words from the Lord Jesus Christ:

"Hereafter I will not talk much with you: for the prince of this world cometh, and hath nothing in me" (John 14:30).

You see, if a thing stays in or with you, then it has found pleasure in you. In the same way we can master this law of favour to influence our attractions, we can also do the same to influence what should not be a part of our lives. Atmospheres will always decide what flourishes or what dies. The Lord Jesus Christ said, **".... he has nothing in me...."** He was not what Satan was attracted to; surely the prince of this world was coming, but he was not going to stay around Him.

The Beauty of Forgiveness

Forgiveness is self-sanctification. Forgiveness does not first do good to anyone else but to yourself. Forgiveness is washing yourself free from the hurt, lest you keep in you things in the likeness of that which bitterness attracts. Remember, something has to find its kind in you to be attracted to you or to stay. Unforgiveness is self-pollution; it keeps in a person that which evil is attracted to. There are people who have kept their lives so polluted with bitterness and unforgiveness that no good thing seems to be attracted to them anymore; no matter how hard they try to make progress, life does not turn out good and interesting.

Forgiveness is not an emotional decision. It is not a decision you make because it feels good; no. It is a wise decision of your own good. There is never a justified reason not to forgive. When you understand the evil unforgiveness brings on you and the good it deprives you of, you will not want to let it stay a moment in you. It is like someone walking on the road, and a car (intentionally or unintentionally) splashes water on him; he gets mad and says he is not going to clean himself up until the driver apologizes. Whether or not he apologizes, will you not clean up? Is refusing to clean up acting wisely? Certainly not. Soon enough, such a person will begin to stink as his dirty clothes and body begin attracting germs and other destructive things which delight in dirt. You see that forgiveness does good to you first, before the person in error.

The Bible says,

"… the dark places of the earth are full of the habitations of cruelty" (Psalms 74:20).

Do you see what dark places attract? If you do not want cruelty, light yourself up. Cruelty is only attracted to dark places. *Unforgiveness is keeping your heart dark, meanwhile, forgiveness is lighting up your heart so that you keep attracting the good things of life and walking in Gods favour.* Think about this. So, there is never a justified reason for not forgiving; it has nothing to do with how you feel about it. Forgiveness first works out personal good.

Forgiveness keeps a person excelling in God's grace, regardless of what is done against the person. If you would refuse to "have in you" what Satan likes, he will have no space in your life. That is why the verse we read earlier said, **"…if you shall purge yourself from these things…."** So, you see, this is not referring to forgiveness only, but any other sin (or weights of life) which seek to pollute our lives and create a dark enough atmosphere for cruelty, instead of the beauty of God's love.

That is why Paul the apostle said,

"For ye know what commandments we gave you by the Lord Jesus. For this is the will of God, even your sanctification, that ye should abstain from fornication: <u>That every one of you should know how to possess his vessel in sanctification and honour;</u> Not in the lust of concupiscence, even as the Gentiles which know not God:" (1 Thessalonians 4:2-5).

If you possess your vessel (your body) in sanctification and in honour, then you are making yourself a lighthouse which only attracts and makes manifest the glory of God. That is why we saw in Chapter One that instead of focusing on the thing you want or do not want, focus on changing your atmosphere. We stink like the atmosphere around us. In other words, our atmospheres reveal who we are and what we have. *To change our atmospheres, we fundamentally change ourselves! We change who we are.* When our atmosphere changes, there are things which will leave and others will come of their own accord. Let go of the stinking meat; it will stop the stench and the flies will leave. So, instead of dealing with the flies, deal with the smell. Isn't this wonderful? What an easy way to live! Ask the Lord to deal with those areas in your life which are unpleasant to Him, and reveal to you that which is glorious and worth putting on.

CHAPTER THREE

THE REVELATION OF YOUR ATMOSPHERE

The Place

The concept is simple; *where you are (place), decides what seasons can occur or are available to you.* Seasons reveal what activities are required, and atmospheres reveal what season it is. So, we have place, season, and atmosphere. Remember, the Word of God speaks in this light saying,

"While the earth remaineth, seedtime and harvest, and cold and heat, and summer and winter, and day and night shall not cease" (Genesis 8:22).

In other words, if you are on earth (place), then seedtime and harvest (activity), cold and heat (atmosphere), and summer and winter (seasons) shall not cease. This is very important for our understanding of how an atmosphere is created or comes about. The first thing a man must therefore identify in order to bring forth profitable changes in his life, is "the place". The question

"Where?" is fundamental to what becomes of a man's atmosphere. In the verse above, the Lord God was saying, "earth" is the place where the activity of seedtime and harvest will always be required to bring forth a man's changes. "While THE EARTH remaineth…" He said. When the place is known, then the right activities are required within the right seasons to produce the right results or experiences.

Seasons occur in places. When you do not know the place, you will be able to identify the seasons that occur there. It is possible for winter to occur anywhere; however, that is decided by the state of the place or the activities therein. *Seasons do not decide places, rather, places decide seasons.* In other words, the activity in the place will decide what seasons occur or cease to occur within a specific geographical area.

As earlier mentioned, your body is a place, your relationship is a place, your job is a place, your business is a place, your academics is a place, etc. There are physical, spiritual, and virtual places in life. Understanding the principles of physical places (like the earth), is fundamental to understanding how spiritual or virtual places work. *Physical things mirror spiritual things.* The fundamental activities that are carried out in these places, will decide what seasons occur there. For example, a mature female body (place), has seasons called, the menstrual cycle. There is a season in which the female body becomes fertile and ready for seed, and there is a season wherein the seed will just be wasted—*it will produce any harvest.* Therefore, knowing the place will tell us what seasons to expect and will enable us take advantage for productivity.

A man's place decides the seasons available to him. To expect a certain season at the wrong place is tantamount to disappointment. There are certain things which only happen in a particular place. And there are certain seasons which may never occur at a given place, except the conditions are met. *Knowing where you are, or where a person is, is fundamental to making profitable investments.* The very first thing a wise person does to live right or make the right decisions is to answer the place question, "Where am I? Where is he or she? Where is it?" When place is sure, then the season question can follow. Geographers and farmers are very much acquainted with such knowledge. Remember, the physical things mirror the spiritual and virtual. Understanding this makes it easy to understand many other areas of life.

The Season

The Bible says,

"To every thing there is a season, and a time to every purpose under the heaven…" (Ecclesiastes 3:1).

This verse is comforting and instructive. As long as a man lives "under heaven", everything is restricted to seasons; everything happens only within its set time and season. "To everything there is a season" also means God has set an expiring date to every purpose; everything only last for just as long as their seasons permit. So, under heaven (or upon the earth), nothing is meant to last forever; everything purpose is restricted to its time.

This gives us hope in life, when we master the purpose of seasons. Upon the earth, seasons guarantee change, and seasons do not last forever. This gives every man the opportunity to expect and to create change. If faced with an unfavourable experience, there is hope, because as long as seasons change, it will not last. *As long as hope keeps us standing, the difficulty will pass with the passing of the season, or a new season will give us an opportunity to effect a favourable change.* As seasons decide what new things come forth, they also decide what things expire. Seasons give life the opportunity for things to start and for things to stop.

A wise heart does not hate seasons; it plans with seasons. In winter, we get pullovers, and in summer we keep them, because we know winter is coming again. A wise heart does not desperately lament over his experiences; it waits for due season and responds accordingly. Genesis 8:22 says, as long as the earth remains, seedtime and harvest shall not cease. In other words, if you missed seedtime or harvest, it will come again. It says cold and heat, summer and winter shall not cease. Therefore, if things are cold now, they will get hot soon; if they are gloomy now in winter, beauty will soon be here in summer. It says day and night shall not cease. So, if you are experiencing darkness now, be hopeful; day will soon come. We have seen this word of God stand true ever since we were born; we have neither had day nor night forever. The natural things of God teach us how well we can manage our lives if we understand God's purpose.

Seasons will always change; seasons will always come. That is to mean, we can always be hopeful. If we understand seasons, plan and act accordingly, we will see that they were not given to work against us, but for us. Atmospheres indicate what seasons are active, and these seasons tell what activities ought to be done (seedtime or harvest). Of course, there are two categories of activities within every season—*sowing or harvesting*, with other minor activities occurring in-between, such as tilling, weeding, spraying, etc. It is said,

"The sluggard will not plow by reason of the cold; therefore shall he beg in harvest, and have nothing" (Proverbs 20:4).

Failure to understand seasons will be failure to master changes in life. *Seasons are favourable times wherein specific factors are made consistent for the pursuit of a given objective.* Seasons are of no consequence, unless you know exactly what to do or what to pursue within the season. The purpose of seasons is to make the activity of seeding and harvesting productive. One season signals that the soil is ready, and the other signals that the harvest is ready (seeds have attained maturity).

That is what the verse we just read above says; the sluggard who "…will not plow by reason of the cold …shall beg in harvest…" The ploughing season was meant for receiving seeds; the cold was necessary for the success of the activity. And because this man refused to honour the purpose of that season, the next season (which was meant to reflect his diligence in the preceding season) would be a disappointment to him. *It is not enough to know the seasons; you must respond accordingly*. Our lives are basically a reflection of our attitude towards seasons.

Remember we saw earlier how the Bible described the children of Issachar; they were "…**men that had understanding of the times, to know what Israel ought to do…**" (1 Chronicles 12:32). 'The times' there refers to the seasons; these men were able to observe the changes in the atmosphere, to know what season it was, and what ought to be done within that season, if a certain experience or change was to come forth.

One of the greatest understanding on earth that can cause anyone to live a smooth life in God's purpose, is the understanding of sequence, protocol, process, and procedures. What ought to come first? What is the sequence of activities which must take place before we can expect a certain change? Those are the questions of a wise heart. That is why the Lord said, "…**seek ye first…**" (Matthew 6:33). That speaks of sequence or order; it was a direct correction of the wrong priorities of man, which are a consequence of a poor understanding of place, season, atmosphere, and activity.

At one time, the siblings of the Lord Jesus Christ asked Him to go up to the feast at Judea (Place), but He answered them saying:

"Go ye up unto this feast: I go not up yet unto this feast; for <u>my time is not yet full come</u>" (John 7:8).

Until the time is right, anything a man does is going to be frustrating and work against him or even against others. Remember how atmosphere matters to influence. The Lord Jesus Christ understood this. He knew that places have seasons, seeds need their seasons, and seeds must be allowed to fully grow before the harvest can be beautiful. Unfortunately, this was not the understanding His siblings had. He had earlier told them,

"…My time is not yet come: but your time is always ready" (John 7:6).

What did He mean by "…*your time is always ready*"? In other words, they did anything at any time; anytime for them was the right time to do whatsoever they wanted; they did not understand the wisdom of first things first. As a result, they never got God's kind of results. For God makes all things beautiful only in His time. So, the Lord Jesus Christ did not just have to wait for His time to come, but for it to fully come. That speaks of a due season indeed. Even God will not break this principle that governs all things; He has submitted Himself to His own Word. The Bible says that even Jesus Christ was born on time; He came at the time He was supposed to come; He came in due season, when the soil was ready to receive Him as a seed, for the new creation to come forth as God's harvest. Jesus came at a time when the necessary factors were made consistent for the success of His assignment, mission, or purpose.

"But when the fulness of the time was come, God sent forth his Son, made of a woman, made under the law, …" (Galatians 4:4).

Glory to God! Think of what this understanding can make of your life. The Son of God (the Seed of God) was on time; He had to be on time, otherwise, He would have been out of season and His death would not have been profitable. In fact, there would not have been a resurrection or a profitable resurrection. Concerning His death, Jesus said,

"Verily, verily, I say unto you, Except a corn of wheat fall into the ground and die, it abideth alone: but if it die, it bringeth forth much fruit" (John 12:24).

Yes, He was that "corn of wheat" which had to fall into the ground and die. But that was not supposed to happen out of season; He waited for His season. When it came, He knew it was the right time to act. Only when He "fell into the ground" on time, did He bring forth much fruit by His resurrection. Halleluiah! Everything beautiful in life follows this blessed order. Seedtime is the season which demands a seed, and harvest time is the season which demands a joyful reception. A joyful reception because that which was sown has been multiplied back to the sower; it has been glorified.

Seasons are not Democratic

Regardless of the quality of a man's seed, a wrong season makes it powerless. *Understanding seasons makes a man set the right expectations, commit to the right activities, and get the right results.* For all things are only beautiful in "His" time—*the time God has ordained for all things to be rightly set, in order to maximize seed and bring forth a harvest beneficial to man.* Activities are not profitable at just anytime. Some words or counsels will not be profitable if offered out of season, no matter how good they are. Giving at the wrong time will be a waste; it must be done in due season. The wealthiest businessmen in the world have as primary advantage, the mastery of seasons. *The most satisfying and fulfilling lives and purposes on earth work and walk within due seasons; they experience the beauty of life by adhering to and respecting their seasons.* A man's Return On Investment (ROI) is going to be proportional to his respect of seasons. This is the understanding the children of Issachar had; they were not going to do things at the wrong time; they were neither ahead of time nor behind time. It is said, they *"…knew what Israel ought to do…"* at a given time (season).

Expecting something good when it is not the season will lead to disappointments. If you are ignorant of the fact that it takes five steps to get a given result, you risk expecting the experience at the second or third step, and you may give up when the results are not forthcoming. And sometimes, you may even give up at the fourth step, wearied by the faulty expectations from the previous steps. A blessed man is one who understands that this success demands five major steps; he only expects beauty at the end of the fifth step.

God is a God of sequence and order. Certain things must take place before an expected result comes forth, if it is going to reveal its true beauty and be beneficial to a man or to a people. There is a reason why it takes nine months to have a full grown baby. Every day counts. If the results are going to be beautiful, the mother would be wise to only begin expecting that from the ninth month. Anything forced out of its time will lose its true beauty, unless it is alternatively subjected to complete its time. That is the reason some babies go back into the incubator, for an artificial completion of their time so that beauty can fully emerge.

Do you see why God is not a democratic God? Democracy can make changes out of season, causing harm both to the majority and minority. God is a right God; He expects that every change should be done within the protocol and sequence required. *Order is fundamental to beauty*. To be beautiful means a thing is in the state in which it fully reveals and fulfils its purpose. It refers to that which is truly profitable to man, according to God's design. Beauty means, to possess and to express the exact qualities expected by the author.

Our Lord Jesus Christ emphasised the need to adhere to the sequence or order in our pursuit of purpose saying,

"For the earth bringeth forth fruit of herself; first the blade, then the ear, after that the full corn in the ear" (Mark 4:28).

In other words, do not expect the full corn, until you have allowed the blade to form, and seen the ear. Only when these two have been fully formed, can you expect the full corn to show up. To expect the full corn from just the level of the blade is to live a life of disappointments, because you will be abusing sequence. The same applies our subject. Every one of us is subject to place, season, and atmosphere, as fundamental requirements to experiencing good changes. *Not knowing where you are, will result in not knowing what seasons to expect. And not knowing what seasons to expect, results in not knowing the meaning of a given atmosphere.* You might know what to do, but you risk not getting the best results without knowing the atmosphere. This understanding can be applied to every of man's pursuit. Places, seasons, and atmospheres are key prerequisites to a successful pursuit.

The Atmosphere

Mastering your changes requires basic mastery of places, seasons, and atmospheres. A lot can be told from a person's atmosphere. The Lord Jesus Christ said:

"… Behold the fig tree, and all the trees; When they now shoot forth, ye see and know of your own selves that summer is now nigh at hand" (Luke 21:29/30).

In other words, observing certain changes will tell you what season you are in. These changes define the atmosphere, which indicates what season it is and consequently what activity is required or expected. In fact, atmospheres are proofs of what the season is. Just as trees are known by their fruits, seasons are known by their atmospheres.

Seasons cannot hide upon the earth. Otherwise, the life of men will be full of trial and error; there will be no mastery of changes and experiences. That is not how God made life to be. *God made life in a way that men are able to understand the best time to do the right thing, in order to get the beautiful results that He desires.* Atmospheres are a season's aroma or fragrance. As God has given us the wisdom to tell a tree by its fruits, even so, has He given us atmospheres to be able to tell seasons. We do not only look at the fig tree to tell that it is summer, but we can also feel the transition of seasons by the state of the atmosphere. Seasons announce themselves by their atmospheres.

In actual fact, within the natural realm of life, atmospheres can be perceived by all of our five senses. The least of men can perceive seasons in order to pursue the best of purpose. *There is something you can see, hear, feel, taste, and smell in order to tell the atmosphere, and as a consequence know what the season is*. People often say, "I smell summer." Every atmosphere has a fragrance, which comes from the existing season. This is the unique fragrance that comes forth when a season is ready for a certain activity. Seasons cannot hide; atmospheres betray them. Selah. This is very important because these are the factors people and things can perceive to tell your atmosphere. Consequently, they would know how to respond towards you; whether to seed into your life or harvest from it. Again, you see how the law of favour works here.

Remember, you are a place, you have seasons, and you carry an atmosphere at all times. *That is to mean, if you can change "your place", you have decided your seasons. With your seasons come your atmospheres. And if you can influence your atmosphere, you are indirectly influencing how men and things react towards you.* It is justified then to say, changing your place is the most basic change to make, to indirectly influence what seasons you can experience. Influencing your season is directly influencing your atmosphere. Seasons are unknown until the atmosphere changes, because the atmosphere is the fruit of the season. While your progression in influence goes from place, season, and then to atmosphere, the reaction of others towards you begins by them identifying your atmosphere, your season, and then your place. *In other words, people determine your atmosphere in order to know your season and your place.* No one wants to sow in a barren land or to sow out of season. Selah.

It is also worth noting that these atmospheres are not just exclusive to what can be perceived by the five senses, for there also exist spiritual atmospheres; these are atmospheres not perceivable by the five senses, but by the spirit; they can only be spiritually discerned. As a matter of fact, we have four major categories of atmospheres which a person can have or be influenced by:

Natural Atmospheres

Natural atmospheres are the atmospheres given by God to all men; they happen to all men, and can be perceived, experienced and maximized by all men. These are the basic atmospheres that govern the earth by virtue of sunrise and sunset (*or the orbit of the earth around the sun*) making for day and night. These atmospheres are decided by the different natural seasons—*winter, spring, summer, and autumn.* They are standard expressions of God's love for all, irrespective of race, colour, country, or age.

"That ye may be the children of your Father which is in heaven: <u>for he maketh his sun to rise on the evil and on the good, and sendeth rain on the just and on the unjust</u>" (Matthew 5:45).

God causing His "sun to rise on the evil and the good, and sending rain on the just and the unjust", speaks of the unbiased love of God extended to all and available for the good of all. Atmospheres from the natural seasons give every man the opportunity to live a good life by virtue of what they make of them. These are atmospheres common to all upon the earth (based on geographical location and activity), which we can take advantage of in order to excel in one pursuit or another.

As natural as these atmospheres are, they can also be influenced or corrupted by human activities. Earlier, we saw how the use of Cloud Seeding Technology (CST) can be used to manipulate or influence the atmosphere, so that it can rain; this comes in to assist or bypass the natural process by which clouds are seeded. If man can manipulate the clouds so that it rains, he can also manipulate the clouds to keep it from raining. That would mean the sons of God can also be at the mercy of the wisdom of men. And that would be disastrous. As wisdom says,

"…God hath made man upright; but they have sought out many inventions" (Ecclesiastes 7:29).

In other words, man has deviated from God's own standard of uprightness. When a man is subject to God indeed, God has a way of bypassing these natural seasons to the glory of His name. We see the case of Isaac as a good example. He overlooked the message behind the natural atmosphere and superimposed the spiritual atmosphere over it. He overruled the natural atmosphere by sowing to the Spirit and prevailed in the plans and purposes of God for his life.

"And there was a famine in the land, …Then Isaac sowed in that land, and received in the same year an hundredfold: and

the LORD blessed him. And the man waxed great, and went forward, and grew until he became very great:" (Genesis 26:1, 12/13).

"Famine in the land" meant the natural season was not favourable; yet, by obeying God's Word, Isaac ascended above the natural season. This is an example of a man who was not limited by the dictates of the natural atmosphere, but by the spiritual (which we will see later on). The natural atmosphere is subject to the spiritual by your walk in faith as a son of God.

World Atmospheres

World atmospheres are those created by activities in the world such as social, economic, political, etc. These can be relative to a given people, a city, or a nation. They are the atmospheres which are influenced by human ideologies, philosophies, opinions, and traditions. This is the world that the Lord Jesus Christ said we are not a part of; we are not exclusively dependent on or influenced by this world, because it is managed or governed by men. Consequently, they have decisions, laws, and systems which may not be in honour of God or consistent with the kingdom of God and His will for His children. This is the world that can be influenced and be corrupted by the adversary.

"They are not of the world, even as I am not of the world" (John 17:16).

So, to live a life dependent on these "worldly atmospheres" is to be trapped, driven, and limited by the seasons of the world and not God's seasons. Since atmospheres influence what comes and what leaves, you will be limited within the experiences of mere men, and not walk in the perfect will of God the Father as a son of God.

Remember, atmospheres reveal seasons, and seasons reveal possibilities. Economic crises, pandemics, and political uproars can be limiting to a people who are exclusively given to worldly atmospheres. The sons of God can live above this. We see the example of Paul and Silas; how they were able to superimpose the divine atmosphere over the worldly by sowing to the Spirit. It is said,

"And at midnight Paul and Silas prayed, and sang praises unto God: and the prisoners heard them. And suddenly there was a great earthquake, so that the foundations of the prison were shaken: and immediately all the doors were opened, and every one's bands were loosed" (Acts 16:25/26).

It was evident that there was an atmosphere superior to that of the world. In other words, the decision of men to keep them bound was confounded. God's ways give His children the advantage over such atmospheres and seasons of the world. Like the LORD puts it,

"Oh that my people had hearkened unto me, and Israel had walked in my ways! I should soon have subdued their

enemies, and turned my hand against their adversaries. The haters of the **LORD** should have submitted themselves unto him: but their time should have endured for ever. He should have fed them also with the finest of the wheat: and <u>with honey out of the rock should I have satisfied thee</u>" (Psalms 81:13-16).

"Honey out of the rock"? Well, that was what God was able to do if His people had listened to Him; He could lead them in glory beyond the atmosphere and seasons of the world. We see how the Lord Jesus Christ ascended above such limitations, when He fed five thousand with just five loaves and two fish. That is to mean, regardless of the economic situation, He was still going to accomplish God's goodwill. Think about that. Though we have such worldly seasons and atmospheres governed and managed by men, God is not limited to that. My book "Sowing to the Spirit" teaches more along this line.

Human Atmospheres

Human atmospheres are atmospheres that reveal a man's personal season based on his age, state of his five senses, or stature; they are influenced by a person's natural activities, personality, presentation, qualification, background, profession, riches, education, etc. These atmospheres are relative to every individual but common to men. In fact, they are those atmospheres we create by our own personal preferences and experiences as humans, which determines how people react towards us and how we react towards them. All of these come from the state of a man's heart and the use of the senses, because a man lives according to the state and quality of his heart. This is the atmosphere which almost made Samuel the prophet to anoint David's brother as king instead of David:

But the LORD said unto Samuel, <u>Look not on his countenance, or on the height of his stature;</u> because I have refused him: for the LORD seeth not as man seeth; for man looketh on the outward appearance, but the LORD looketh on the heart (1 Samuel 16:7).

These atmospheres can be deceptive, because they are conditioned by men. That is why Paul the apostle said, we walk by faith and not by sight. David did not look like a king; his brother did. If it was left to human atmospheres, as important as they can be, he would not have been chosen even by Samuel the prophet. Sons live beyond human atmospheres; they judge in righteousness, that is, from the Father's Word and Spirit.

Favour is deceitful, and beauty is vain: but a woman that feareth the LORD, she shall be praised (Proverbs 31:30).

"Favour" in this verse speaks of that which we have the tendency to respond kindly to because of how well we feel about it, based on our sensual perceptions and judgements. Abraham knew how to overlook this atmopshere and walk in God's perfect will for his life; he waved its influence and sowed to the Spirit, and received the Spirit's harvest.

And being not weak in faith, he considered not his own body now dead, when he was about an hundred years old, neither yet the deadness of Sara's womb: He staggered not at the promise of God through unbelief; but was strong in faith, giving glory to God; And being fully persuaded that, what he had promised, he was able also to perform. And therefore it was imputed to him for righteousness (Romans 4:19-22).

It is said, "…. he considered not his own body now dead, when he was about an hundred years old, neither yet the deadness of Sara's womb…" Halleluiah! That was a man who had ascended above depending on mere sensory perceptions; he refused to accept the natural evidence of impossibility as truth, and rather chose to stick to God's Word. That gave him a different place, a different season, and a different atmosphere. His judgment of life ascended beyond what is seen and heard, just as it was said of our Lord Jesus Christ:

And the spirit of the LORD shall rest upon him, the spirit of wisdom and understanding, the spirit of counsel and might, the spirit of knowledge and of the fear of the LORD; And shall make him of quick understanding in the fear of the LORD: and <u>he shall not judge after the sight of his eyes, neither reprove after the hearing of his ears</u>: (Isaiah 11:2/3).

There was something exceptional about our Lord Jesus Christ. By virtue of the spirit that operated in His life, He had a quick understanding in the fear of the Lord. Consequently, He went past judging based on His sight and reproving based on what he heard. This is how to live past human seasons.

When you understand your place in God, you will realize that you can live higher than human atmospheres created by natural human seasons. There is a life above the influence of mere human atmospheres; it is the heavenly, the divine, or the eternal atmosphere. It is the atmosphere of faith we can ascend to in order to receive that which was not possible within the natural, world, or human seasons and atmospheres. It supersedes the limitations of every other atmosphere or season.

Heavenly Atmospheres

The heavenly atmosphere is the atmosphere influenced by the Word of God; it is the atmosphere that comes into existence upon the earth for a man, when the Word of God rules his heart and life. It is the atmosphere of faith in God. These are atmospheres which occur or are created when a person is yielded to God's Word and is in fellowship with the Holy Spirit. This is the believer's true atmosphere (the atmosphere of the sons of God); an atmosphere superior to the natural, world, and human atmospheres. You can call it the kingdom or spiritual atmosphere. Such atmospheres make a person's life consistent with God's will, regardless of the state of the above four atmospheres. It is the dominant atmosphere which rules every other atmosphere and makes manifest the perfect will of God in the life of a person or a people. It can overrule every one of the atmospheres we have seen thus far. It is the atmosphere created when a person not only lives in the Spirit, but also walks in the Spirit. It is the reason Paul the apostle says,

"If we live in the Spirit, let us also walk in the Spirit" (Galatians 5:25).

This atmosphere makes you live a life exempt from worldly atmospheres. It makes the sons of God flourish at all times, because it is not restricted by the limitations of other atmospheres which are subject to human influence and corruption. This is the atmosphere of those who fear the Lord; it is an incorruptible atmosphere because the place is only accessible by God Himself and the seasons are divine. The man with this atmosphere is said to be…

"… like a tree planted by the rivers of water, that bringeth forth his fruit in his season; his leaf also shall not wither; and whatsoever he doeth shall prosper" (Psalms 1:3).

Did you notice that such a man has a different "place"? It is one "by the rivers of water"; that is his flourishing place; it decides his seasons, and consequently his heavenly atmosphere. Halleluiah! Such a man lives a different life, flourishing when others may be stranded and stagnant; he is preserved when others may be destroyed and blown off; he is supplied when others may be starving. The Bible describes a man with such a divine positioning and atmosphere, saying,

"When men are cast down, then thou shalt say, There is lifting up; and he shall save the humble person" (Job 22:29).

Remember, comparing a man with a contrary experience to this man with a heavenly atmosphere, the Psalmist says,

"The ungodly are not so: but are like the chaff which the wind driveth away. Therefore the ungodly shall not stand in the judgment, nor sinners in the congregation of the righteous" (Psalms 1:4/5).

We see that there is a difference of place between these men. The latter is not found in the congregation of the righteous. In other words, they do not have the same atmosphere. Consequently, they do not have the same results. The heavenly atmosphere is one experienced by a man who dwells in the presence of the Lord—*in the secret place*. It is said,

"He that dwelleth in the secret place of the most High shall abide under the shadow of the Almighty. I will say of the LORD, He is my refuge and my fortress: my God; in him will I trust" (Psalms 91:1/2).

That is the beauty of the heavenly atmosphere; it is the faith atmosphere, the spiritual atmosphere, the kingdom atmosphere. This atmosphere is superior in effect and is the permanent atmosphere of the sons of God. By having such an atmosphere as the righteous, you will be able to say, *"The Lord is my refuge and my fortress; my God; in Him will I trust."* That cannot be said by those who are ignorant of this atmosphere; rather, they are driven by the wind; their lives and affairs are unstable, tossed to and fro by the corruption and limitation of natural, world, and human seasons. The heavenly atmosphere is the believer's atmosphere.

The Activity

So far, we have broken down the wisdom behind Genesis 8:22, which says,

"While the earth remaineth, <u>seedtime and harvest</u>, and cold and heat, and summer and winter, and day and night shall not cease."

We have seen the earth (the place), atmosphere (cold and heat), summer and winter (the season), and now, seedtime and harvest (the activity). "Seedtime and harvest" speaks of the activities necessary within a given season; it speaks of the cause and effect activity. Seasons are of none effect to a person unless the right activity is carried out. The very first activity is the seedtime. This is the season or the time where "a place" receives seeds. As said earlier, your body is a place, just as your heart is. At any given time, you are either sowing into one of these—*your body or your heart.*

Success is not attained by the mere consciousness of the available season, but as a result of carrying out the right activity within the season.

If we take our bodies for example, and agree that the body is a place, then we understand that eating is the way we sow to our bodies. When we do that, we wait for another season called harvest, which also permits us engage in an activity called harvesting (that is receiving the results of sown seeds); our bodies do that automatically. We can tell the quality of that harvest either by our level of strength or by our state of health.

Harvest is when the nutrients from your food are absorbed by your body to make the body stronger or healthier; it may just produce more strength, or heal damaged tissues or parts of the body. Strength and health are the harvests of good feeding, while weakness or ill-health is the harvest of poor feeding. The state of your body (harvest) can reveal what seeds you have been sowing into it. We can then conclude that strength or weakness; health or sickness, are proves of the activity carried out in season towards our bodies.

Emotions are harvests; everything we feel is the result of a seed sown into us; either by us or by someone else. There is no emotion without a cause, just as there is no harvest without a seed. In eating (sowing to our bodies), we can also get the harvest of an emotion, which sometimes can also be faulty. You can feel good about what eventually destroys you. Some seeds we sow produce their harvest sooner than others. Gout for example—*known to be caused by feeding your body with too much meat*— often produces its harvest much later in life; it has an age (which is the season) of harvest.

The beauty in having a wise heart is that it is able to discern both time and judgment, as we saw earlier. What that means is, a wise heart knows seasons, knows the seed, and what to expect of that seed sooner or later. A harvest is not strange to a wise person; he knows what seed brings forth a certain harvest. When you understand this, you will give careful attention to the seeds you sow or are sowing in life, for after seedtime comes the harvest. Because some people may not have such wise judgment, they get surprised sooner or later when their harvest shows up; they are unable to tell when they sowed a certain seed into their lives or into that of others.

Every experience we have in life is a harvest; there is none that can exist except it is a harvest of a known or unknown seed. Sometimes, these seeds are sown by us, and sometimes they are sown by others. *Emotions are harvests of sown thoughts.* These thoughts are communicated into us via words. What we hear produces the corresponding emotion, and inspires what becomes of our next seed (or activity). For as much as emotions are harvests, they can also become a cause for us to act and get another reaction as a harvest.

As food is to the body, so are words to a man's heart. Remember, the sower who went out to sow in Mark Chapter 4 sowed the Word of God. The Word of God was the seed sown into hearts, which brought forth the harvest; some thirty, some sixty, and some a hundred. By that, we see that a harvest is multiplication of a seed. This is very important. The time between seedtime and harvest is the time necessary for the seed to multiply its effect. *Therefore, if you know the seed, you can make the best judgment if you want that multiplied in your life or not.* This is how God increases His glory in His children; it is also how Satan multiplies his wickedness in those who open up to him. Because words create our experiences by multiplying in us, the Lord Jesus Christ said:

"… Take heed what ye hear: with what measure ye mete, it shall be measured to you: and unto you that hear shall more be given" (Mark 4:24).

What did He mean by "…with what measure you mete, it shall be measured to you…"? He meant every man will be a product of the words he receives into his heart. And in the likeness of the words, shall his harvest be. That is the law of proportionality; you can decide your measure of harvest by the measure of your investment. Just as Paul the apostle said,

"Be not deceived; God is not mocked: for whatsoever a man soweth, that shall he also reap" (Galatians 6:7).

And again,

"… He which soweth sparingly shall reap also sparingly; and he which soweth bountifully shall reap also bountifully" (2 Corinthians 9:6).

Since seeds multiply their effect within seedtime and harvest, the Lord Jesus Christ said: "…**and unto you that hear shall more be given…**" How will more be given? More will be given through the harvest! So, hearing is receiving what is spoken into your heart, and letting it stay there to the point where it influences your actions, conduct, activities, or way of life. If you hear (receive into your heart and let it stay there), then it is obvious that you have sown into your heart, and so the harvest is the season of more. This is a generic principle which works out both good and evil in the lives of men. That is the reason for the caution, "…*take heed what you hear*…" Those words from the Lord are to be treated seriously. *If you do not want a certain harvest (result or experience), then do not sow the seeds. If you want a harvest, then sow the seeds.* The caution is "take heed"; give attention to this so that you can master your experiences by choosing your seeds wisely.

Wisdom says,

"Keep thy heart with all diligence; for out of it are the issues of life" (Proverbs 4:23).

The phrase "Issues of life" speaks of the experiences of life. That is some serious cautioning again similar to that given by the Lord Jesus Christ. What goes in is what will come out in multiplied effect. To take control of your experiences, take control of the activities carried out within your fertile seasons; they decide what becomes of your harvest.

What is the current state of your health, emotions, relationships, ministry, or business? They are revealing the seeds (your activity during your seedtime). You can change it by identifying your season, identifying the necessary seed, and then getting involved in the right activity. The distinction of the believer comes when he has an understanding of his unique place, season, atmosphere, and activity. It is the activity of the believer within a given season that makes for the believer's kind of results.

CHAPTER FOUR

THE BELIEVER

Who is a Believer?

In a generic sense, everyone is a believer because everyone believes something and is a product of his beliefs. When we speak of a believer from a biblical perspective, we speak of someone who has received (accepted and lives by) the gospel of Jesus Christ; someone who has heard the gospel and received the witness of the Holy Spirit that he is a son of God, born through the resurrection of Jesus Christ from the dead. This is a believer; a person whose trust rests on the faith of Christ, and not in his own works. So, the author of Hebrews says,

"Looking unto Jesus the author and finisher of our faith; who for the joy that was set before him endured the cross, despising the shame, and is set down at the right hand of the throne of God" (Hebrews 12:2).

Whenever the gospel is preached, it fundamentally seeks to make a person to believe. Believing will decide what becomes of a man's life, thoughts, priorities, and pursuits. That is what the gospel of Jesus Christ basically seeks to accomplish. Paul the apostle says,

"… if thou shalt confess with thy mouth the Lord Jesus, <u>and shalt believe in thine heart</u> that God hath raised him from the dead, thou shalt be saved. <u>For with the heart man believeth unto righteousness</u>; and with the mouth confession is made unto salvation" (Romans 10:9/10).

"…shalt believe in thine heart…" "…for with the heart man believes…" Therefore, believers are those who have responded from their hearts to the message of Christ that was preached to them. A complete message includes who Christ is, what He has done, and your new status in the Father's love. The gospel contains all of these, and preaching is the primary way via which it is communicated to a person.

Paul the apostle expresses his trust in the gospel saying,

"For I am not ashamed of the gospel of Christ: for it is the power of God unto <u>salvation to every one that believeth</u>; to the Jew first, and also to the Greek" (Romans 1:16).

Did you notice that this salvation is for "everyone who believes"? We begin to see from here just how fundamental believing is to a man's "salvation"— *the experience of the liberty and life of Christ.* What differentiates two people is their belief. It is worth noting that knowledge is the base of every man's belief. That is why the gospel of Christ is a message which presents a person with knowledge that is worth believing. A man's belief decides his response to life; it decides what things are possible to him and the things that have access to his life. The ability to believe is given to all men to enable them choose their experiences. Knowledge is always a proposal or a call. Men answer by believing. *Every man's belief system is a God-given power of restriction and control, given to him to decide what to receive or to reject.*

In the book of Acts, precisely Chapter 5 v. 14, those who had received the gospel of the Lord Jesus Christ were called believers:

"And <u>believers were the more added to the Lord,</u> multitudes both of men and women"

Paul the apostle speaking to Timothy also said,

"Let no man despise thy youth; but be thou <u>an example of the believers,</u> in word, in conversation, in charity, in spirit, in faith, in purity" (1 Timothy 4:12).

We see then that a certain group of people were called believers; they had believed the gospel of Jesus Christ, and as a result had a certain conduct. Their experiences were reflective of their belief.

The Heart & Belief

"... with the heart man believeth unto righteousness;" (Romans 10:10).

Man's heart in this context, does not refer to the organ that is responsible for pumping blood into the body. The heart here refers to the mind, which is responsible for decision making. Summarily, it is where man's convictions are formed; they are formed by the way he perceives things via all his senses working in unison. From the heart, a man judges whether to accept or to reject. In this context, the heart controls man's belief system; he uses it to either believe or not.

Judgment is the last decision made by a man's belief system after processing information. The end of this process instructs the man to either accept a thing or reject it. Believing would mean accepting and not believing would mean rejecting. This is so peculiar to humans, and has to be understood, for a conscious and wise use of the heart, vis-a-vis the changes a man desires or despises. No man is under compulsion to believe anything. The ability to believe is the wisdom of God placed in all humans to choose, restrict, or control their changes.

Since believing receives or accepts a change and not believing resists or rejects a change, then there must first be an existing image or proposal requiring a man's acceptance or rejection. God's Word is the established truth about us, which provides us with a pure image of ourselves and God the Father, for us to believe.

What is believing?

Believing is becoming one at heart with the image presented via knowledge; it is identifying (becoming identical) by responding in agreement with the image presented via knowledge. That is, at the moment of believing, there is some sort of a merging whereby the believer "possesses" the image, becoming one with it as if imprinted in his mind. From then on, the image governs the believer's thoughts, words, and conduct. In this state, there is no independence between the image and what is believed at heart. We can say believing is owning the image presented by knowledge (through any of the five senses); it is being one or identical with the image. That knowledge (or image) worth believing is the gospel of Christ Jesus.

You will soon see how important this is. For until believing takes place, confession cannot happen or it would be ineffective, empty, and inconsequential.

The Word of God and Belief

The Word of God is the purest form of knowledge that a man can be exposed to. In other words, it is the purest and richest form of knowledge known and available to man. It presents and proposes to a man the most excellent of changes and experiences. So, the Lord Jesus Christ said to Martha, "**... Said I not unto thee, that, IF THOU WOULDEST BELIEVE, thou shouldest see the glory of God?**" (John 11:40). That is a good verse to summarize the purpose and power of believing the Word of God and the experience (the glory) that follows. If Martha would see the glory, then believing was a prerequisite; she had to become one with Christ and His Word, to the point where she consequently acted in the direction of her belief. Remember the purpose of believing is to influence a man's thoughts, words, and conduct.

The understanding of how powerful believing is to a man would drive any man to become mindful of what images (knowledge) he exposes himself to. So, from the time a man receives an image into his heart, he is not far from the change or experience. That is why the Bible cautions us saying,

"Keep thy heart with all diligence; for out of it [are] the issues of life" (Proverbs 4:23).

The first place a man should watch in order to decide his changes, is his heart. For what gets in will eventually influence his belief, and consequently come forth as an experience—*the issues of life*. That verse of wisdom requires that you give careful attention to the images your heart entertains, and by so doing, you will not be ignorant about the changes or experiences in your life.

God's Word brings to us His thoughts. And that is fundamentally how God influences our changes to reflect what He thinks about us. God does not violate a man's belief system; no. He works in harmony with man's right of choice. So, we are told of God's thoughts:

"For I know the thoughts that I think toward you, saith the LORD, thoughts of peace, and not of evil, to give you an expected end" (Jeremiah 29:11).

If God will not violate our right to believe, then giving us His Word is giving us His desired change. How we treat that (by believing or not believing) is up to us. Not having God's Word is being void of godly experiences or changes, because there is no godly image to behold nor to believe (to become one with). So, we see many times across the Bible, God laying so much emphasis on us giving Him our hearts. In Proverbs, He says,

"My son, give me thine heart, and let thine eyes observe my ways." (Proverbs 23:26).

Of course, at this point you know what for. If He does not have your attention, how can He show you what change to receive (believe), given that man understands in pictures. If God gets a man's heart (by getting his attention), then He will influence changes in his life by influencing what he sees and what he eventually believes about himself, life, and circumstances. *All the good that God thinks of us can stay as a desire in God and not become our practical experiences, if our hearts are not given to Him.*

To help "Abram" believe correctly in his future— "Abraham", God asked for Abram's heart. He wanted to show Abram the pictures of the changes which He desired for him; He was bringing Abram into Abraham. Because Abram gave God his attention, the Lord God took him out and showed him the starts to make him believe in Abraham. Halleluiah! Now Abram believed in Abraham, and surely became the father of many nations—*he manifested*

Abraham. Abram merged with the image of Abraham, and in his heart became Abraham (though others still saw him as Abram). It is said,

"…Abraham believed God, and it was counted unto him for righteousness" (Romans 4:3).

By believing in his heart the image (the Word) God showed him, Abram owned Abraham; he became one with Abraham. Praise the Lord! You see, even though it is true that we are made in the righteousness of Christ, it takes the gospel to make us see the picture of what God has done, in order to believe in it. We embrace God's righteousness by believing His righteousness; we become one with it, share in it, and own it by believing. When a man believes, he sees himself in that knowledge. Only then does he give it expression, because he has "owned" the image. You can only give out what you have; you can only live who you are. And as a man thinks in his heart, so is he. (Proverbs 23:7). That is why Paul the apostle said, with the heart man believes unto righteousness. Halleluiah!

God's Word is the mirror of who we are in Him and a mirror of His desired experiences for us. It is said,

"...as we look, we are changed into the same image from glory to glory..." (2 Corinthians 3:18).

Changes will continue to occur if a person remains one with what he sees. It is the same wisdom given to Joshua in Joshua 1:8. Joshua was asked to consciously commit his heart in meditation on God's Word. He was told if he keeps his heart and mouth filled with the Word of God, to the point where he acted accordingly, he would create for himself prosperity and good success. That was a lifetime principle; it was not dispensational. It was not just for Abraham or Joshua, but also for us today:

"This book of the law shall not depart out of thy mouth; but thou shalt meditate therein day and night, that thou mayest observe to do according to all that is written therein: for then thou shalt make thy way prosperous, and then thou shalt have good success" (Joshua 1:8).

Applying these words spoken to Joshua in your life today, will also create for you the same results—*prosperity and good success*. It does not matter what life has been for you, where you have been stagnant or failing; you can also receive a new image in your heart and live it. That is the very first step through which God brings forth His glorious changes in the life of a person; He gets the person to become one at heart with His Word. *Our true, glorious, and incorruptible self is that which God's Word presents us to be.*

In Joshua 1:8 which we just saw, it is amazing to see that the responsibility of change was not given to God but to Joshua. God gave him the change via His Word. It was up to Joshua to give his heart to it, see the image, and become one with it; it was up to him to believe it. That is also to mean the word Joshua was asked to focus on, was the word that would bring him into a life of prosperity and good success. Isn't that wonderful? God showed Joshua the future he could feature in, if he so yielded his heart to it or accepted it. Changes come as a proposal. Whether via a dream or a vision, good or bad; the power to yield and receive, or resist and reject is with you; you are the lord of your changes. God made us masters of our changes when He gave us a heart and a mouth. *If something has no place in your heart, it will have no part in your experiences.*

Triggering or creating your changes is first decided by the content and activities of your heart, which comes as a result of the images (knowledge) you are exposed to. Regardless of what area of change you desire; it has to start from your heart; it starts from the place where no one knows it nor sees it—*in the private quarters of your heart. Right believing is fundamental to right experiences.*

What images do you see in your heart? What are you one with? What have you come to believe about who you are in Christ? What is real in your heart which is yet to become your practical experience? Let God's Word paint the right image in you. God's Word creates and presents His vision in us. Listening to God's Word should be like watching a movie of yourself and life in God's kingdom. See your nature and personality in it; see your mannerism, your path, direction, and changes in it, and be one with what you see. That is believing, receiving, or being one with God. *Believing is receiving the change first in your heart.* By believing, you have a foretaste of what even your physical eyes have a clue about.

The Mouth and Confession

"...with the mouth confession is made unto salvation" (Romans 10:10).

The heart has its distinct function from the mouth, but it is important to master the sequence. The heart does not do the month's job neither does the mouth do the heart's job. But the heart and the mouth are in a sequential partnership, with the heart preceding the mouth. In other words, when the heart is right, and the mouth reflects the same, then changes are set in motion or created. *When it comes to producing changes, words are ineffective without the heart, and the heart will not do much without the mouth. The quality of the mouth is decided by the state of the heart.*

"This people draweth nigh unto me with their mouth, and honoureth me with [their] lips; but their heart is far from me" (Matthew 15:8).

The mouth waits on the heart to be true and effective; *the heart creates the seed and the mouth sows it.* The mouth is in deception if it is not first in sync with the heart; the mouth is empty if the heart is not full. Therefore, the simple rule is: the quality of the mouth is decided by the state of the heart. That is what the Lord Jesus Christ is saying to us in the above verse; that *if we do not get it right from the heart, the mouth will not do much good.* Mastering this is vital to maximizing the believer's atmosphere.

Paul the apostle was mindful of this order when he placed first the heart (for believing) before the mouth (for confession). The order is important. Confessions which do not proceed from a believing heart (a heart one with an image), will not bring forth anything. The Lord Jesus Christ said,

"... for out of the abundance of the heart the mouth speaketh" (Matthew 12:34).

These are core principles for life. Principles, protocols, and procedures reveal to us sequence. *When producing changes, the heart precedes the mouth.* A change in a person's belief system is a delicate change. When that happens, then the mouth can do its own part, for the mouth takes from the heart to bring forth. It is only out of the abundance of the heart that the mouth speaks. Our Lord Jesus Christ emphasizes that again in Matthew 12:34.

Let us once more look at the instructions of wisdom given to Joshua in the book of Joshua 1:8:

"This book of the law shall not depart out of thy mouth; but thou shalt meditate therein day and night, that thou mayest observe to do according to all that is written therein: for then thou shalt make thy way prosperous, and then thou shalt have good success" (Joshua 1:8).

In other words,

"Joshua, you must keep confessing the Word of God (the images given to you about yourself and conduct in God). However, for your words to be effective, to the point where you actually live or do the Word (walk in it) and experience prosperity and good success, you must give yourself to consistent meditation (keeping your mind on the picture)."

So, flowing with the understanding of the mechanics behind creating changes, we see that we receive information via our senses, we believe it (*analyze it and agree with it; become one with it*) at heart, then we confess (*speak and act in line with the Word*). As long as this is done with respect of place and season, the result will be prosperity and good success *—the showing forth of the glory of the Lord.* It is important to understand that a change in personality can influence almost every other thing in your life, because you are what you do. That is why the change from the heart can change how you treat yourself, what you do in your relationships, business, career, etc. The root of this is right believing, and the root of right believing is right knowledge.

The Believer and The Gospel

The gospel presents the finished works (the good, complete, and perfect work) which God has done for all men by Christ Jesus; it reveals the new place and state of all creation—*in Christ*. Thus far, we have established that everyone is a place. "In Christ" speaks of the new creation person. That includes his looks, associations, rights, and privileges by virtue of the redemptive work of God through Christ Jesus; it speaks of the being, made in the likeness of Christ and who shares in all that He (Christ) has and represents. Peter the apostle of Christ speaks of this saying,

"According as his divine power hath given unto us all things that pertain unto life and godliness, through the knowledge of him that hath called us to glory and virtue: Whereby are given unto us exceeding great and precious promises: that <u>by these ye might be partakers of the divine nature</u>, having escaped the corruption that is in the world through lust" (2 Peters 1:3/4).

By the Lord Jesus Christ, God's divine power has made us partakers of the divine nature. That is basically what the gospel presents, which a man has to believe. That is why Paul the apostle says,

"… if any man be in Christ, <u>he is a new creature:</u> old things are passed away; behold, all things are become new" (2 Corinthians 5:17).

We see that he did not say "he will become a new creature"; no. He said, HE IS a new creature. That is the man's current state, which the gospel seeks to make him know, presenting the Lord Jesus Christ as the reason such a change has taken place or has been made possible to men. The Bible teaches us that when He was raised from the dead, we were raised with Him (Ephesians 2:4/5). As we saw earlier, Jesus Christ was the seed that was sown in season, to bring forth a quality harvest; He was wisely invested for a quality return. So, we read,

"For it became him, for whom are all things, and by whom are all things, <u>in bringing many sons unto glory,</u> to make the captain of their salvation perfect through sufferings" (Hebrews 2:10).

Halleluiah! "…in bringing many sons unto glory…" is the harvest. How did this happen? By His death (by being sown) and His resurrection (the harvest). In Christ, the believer has become the fruit or harvest of Christ's investment; the believer is the product (the result) of his suffering. The believer is the glorious outcome of the travail of the soul of Christ, in whom He (Christ) rejoices, just as a woman rejoices when she sees the child of her travail.

"He shall see of the travail of his soul, and shall be satisfied: …" (Isaiah 53:11).

This believer in Christ is not just one created in the image of Christ or who came forth by the resurrection as seen in Ephesians 2:10, but one who has been granted access to the very presence of God the Father—*the secret place*. The following verses shed light on this:

"Jesus saith unto him, I am the way, the truth, and the life: no man <u>cometh unto the Father, but by me</u>" (John 14:6).

If the believer has therefore come through Christ, then the believer now lives in the Father's presence. It goes well with what Paul the apostle said, **"But ye are come unto mount Sion, and unto the city of the living God, the heavenly Jerusalem, and to an innumerable company of angels…"** (Hebrews 12:22).

Seven Key Facts About the Believer:

1. The believer is sanctified by the blood of Christ and justified in God's sight

The following verses attest to that:

"Unto the church of God which is at Corinth, to <u>them that are sanctified in Christ Jesus</u>, called to be saints, with all that in

every place call upon the name of Jesus Christ our Lord, both theirs and ours:" (1 Corinthians 1:2).

"And such were some of you: but <u>ye are washed,</u> but <u>ye are sanctified,</u> but <u>ye are justified</u> in the name of the Lord Jesus, and by the Spirit of our God" (1 Corinthians 6:11).

"For both <u>he that sanctifieth</u> and <u>they who are sanctified</u> are all of one: for which cause he is not ashamed to call them brethren…" (Hebrews 2:11).

To believe in Jesus Christ is to believe in that which the Word says, even the gospel; that in Him a man is sanctified and justified (declared not guilty) in God's sight. This is so important. Christ has become our sanctification.

"That no flesh should glory in his presence. But of him are ye in Christ Jesus, who of God is <u>made unto us</u> wisdom, and righteousness, and <u>sanctification,</u> and redemption:" (1 Corinthians 1:29/30).

Why should no flesh glory (boast) in God's presence? Because Christ is the reason for a man's sanctification, by whom and in whom exists the bold confidence to come before God the Father and to live in His presence. Without Christ being esteemed this way, a man is independent of Christ and is not worthy in himself before God. So, to keep man away from himself, from trusting his frailty, and from self-condemnation, Christ became man's sanctifier. In Him (placed there by God the Father) man is sanctified. In Him here means to be created as unto Christ; He's the sanctifying "accompaniment" of the new creature. The new creature is not and cannot be independent of Christ.

"And you, that were sometime alienated and enemies in your mind by wicked works, yet now hath he reconciled In the body of his flesh through death, <u>to present you holy and unblameable and unreproveable in his sight:</u>" (Colossians 1:21/22).

2. The believer has received God's gift of righteousness

It is God, who by Christ has sanctified and justified the believer, offering Christ as the believer's gift of righteousness. This gives the believer an eternally approved state before God, as long as the believer places faith in Christ and not in himself. It is said,

"For if by one man's offence death reigned by one; much more they which receive abundance of grace and of the gift of righteousness shall reign in life <u>by one, Jesus Christ</u>" (Romans 5:17).

"By one, Jesus Christ" is key to grasping this. The strength of the faith is boldly deserving it, not because of what you have done, but because of what God has done through Christ. As long as a man is righteous, condemnation has lost its legality, thereby giving man the right to reign in life. Consequently, those who have received Christ's righteousness shall reign in life BY ONE JESUS CHRIST. As seen in 1 Corinthians 1:30, Jesus Christ is made unto the believer "Righteousness." In other words, by virtue of being in Christ, Christ has become the believer's standard of being right before God. This gift of righteousness comes from God Himself in the person of Christ Jesus. That is why it is said,

"No weapon that is formed against thee shall prosper; and every tongue that shall rise against thee in judgment thou shalt condemn. This is the heritage of the servants of the LORD, and their righteousness is of me, saith the LORD" (Isaiah 54:17).

The reason the believer has such rights to condemn tongues of judgment or accusations is because his justification (being declared not guilty) is not decided by his works; it is the declaration of God by virtue of the faithfulness of Christ Jesus. This is the grace of God; not of works, lest any man should boast. The reason why it is said, **"…their righteousness is of me, saith the LORD."** This also goes well with what Jeremiah had said regarding these people who will be known as "the chosen generation", saying,

"In his days Judah shall be saved, and Israel shall dwell safely: and this is his name whereby he shall be called, THE LORD OUR RIGHTEOUSNESS" (Jeremiah 23:6).

Then he goes further to say they shall rejoice in this saying,

"The LORD hath brought forth our righteousness: come, and let us declare in Zion the work of the LORD our God" (Jeremiah 51:10).

Amazing! If the believer has been declared by God Himself to be righteousness, who and what then can lay a successful accusation against him, to the point of getting the him condemned to death or destruction? Absolutely nothing and no one, for God is above all. In the light of this gospel, Paul the apostle makes the following emphatic declarations of faith:

"There is therefore now no condemnation to them which are in Christ Jesus, who walk not after the flesh, but after the Spirit. Who shall lay any thing to the charge of God's elect? It is God that justifieth. Who is he that condemneth? It is Christ that died, yea rather, that is risen again, who is even at the right hand of God, who also maketh intercession for us" (Romans 8:1, 33/34).

Praise the Lord! The believer in Christ is associated with God's very own righteousness; there is no room for a successful accusation in God's sight, as long as the believer holds firm to that which God has declared him to be—*the righteousness of God in Christ Jesus.*

3. The believer has become a new creature, and shares in the exact glory of Christ by being in His likeness

The resurrection of Jesus Christ has made the believer a whole new kind of being in the likeness and glory of Christ Jesus. 2 Corinthians 5:17 says, the one in Christ has become a new creature. In other words, this person in Christ is given a new kind of nature, which is the divine and incorruptible nature. It is that which is in the likeness of the resurrected Christ.

Ephesians 2:10 says,

"For we are his workmanship, <u>created in Christ Jesus</u> unto good works, which God hath before ordained that we should walk in them".

It says "…created…" not, will be created. It is the current state of the believer in Christ. Such a person is made in the likeness of Christ. That is what it means to be created in Christ. It goes same to confirm what 2 Corinthians 5:17 says; *"If any man be in Christ (be created in Christ or as unto Christ), then he is a new creature (not will be, but he is)".* That is what the Lord Jesus Christ meant when He said,

"And the glory which thou gavest me <u>I have given them; that they may be one, even as we are one</u>:" (John 17:22).

That teaches us that if we have received the glory of Christ then we are made like Him, to share in His very likeness or divine nature. Halleluiah! This is what believing brings men to share in; it brings us into such a glorious participation in that which we are already made and called to be in Him. You are not an ordinary being or creature in Christ; no. You are of the very divine kind and class. Peter the apostle says,

"Whereby are given unto us exceeding great and precious promises: that by <u>these ye might be partakers of the divine nature,</u> having escaped the corruption that is in the world through lust" (2 Peter 1:4).

Believing in Jesus brings a person to a conscious and a glorious participation in the divine nature. Halleluiah! That is the message in the gospel. It is what the author of the book of Hebrews meant when he said,

"For it became him, for whom are all things, and by whom are all things, <u>in bringing many sons unto glory</u>, to make the captain of their salvation perfect through sufferings" (Hebrews 2:10).

Praise the Lord! He has brought us—*many sons*— unto glory by His resurrection. It is written,

"For ye know the grace of our Lord Jesus Christ, that, though he was rich, yet for your sakes he became poor, <u>that ye through his poverty might be rich</u>" (2 Corinthians 8:9).

What does it mean to be made rich? It means to be a partaker of the divine nature or to share in the glory of Christ. That is who the new creature really is; it speaks of one who shares in the exact glory of Christ; one who shares in the beauty and excellence of the incorruptible life of God in Christ Jesus—*the Son of God.* Believing the gospel causes you to actively share in all that Christ is as a Son of God.

4. The believer shares in the very life of Christ— the eternal life of God, being made a partaker of the divine nature

A man cannot be a new creature in Christ without being a possessor of eternal life—*the very life of Christ.* Being a new creature also means, one who has the eternal life operational in him. Just as in Christ you are not to become a new creature, but you already are a new creature; even so, in Christ, you are not to receive eternal life but you are already a possessor of eternal life; eternal life belongs to you now; it is the very life that you live. That is what God's Word reveals. It is said,

"The thief cometh not, but for to steal, and to kill, and to destroy: I am come that they might have

life, and <u>that they might have it more abundantly</u>" (John 10:10).

So, Christ Jesus came that we might HAVE ABUNDANT (everlasting, incorruptible, indestructible) LIFE. That is the current inheritance of the one who is in Christ. It is so important to understand the qualities of this life to really appreciate what you have received. That is why John said,

"And this is the record, that <u>God hath given to us eternal life</u>, and this life is in his Son" (1 John 5:11).

Did you take note of the tense? "…*God hath given to us eternal life…*" Halleluiah! Not God will give us; but God has given. This removes an attitude of discontentment which can be ignorantly exercised towards God, as though He is still to do something significant. According to God, He has GIVEN us eternal life. Then John tells us where this life is saying, "…*this life is in his Son…*" If that be true, then verse 12 draws the conclusion saying,

"He that hath the Son hath life; and he that hath not the Son of God hath not life."

In other words, he who has believed in Jesus Christ has this life operational in him. This is because he has received God's Son in whom is eternal life. And beyond that, we know that He is life, for

He said "...**I am the way, the truth, and the life**..." (John 14:6). John goes ahead to tell us the reason why he is saying all this:

"These things have I written unto you that believe on the name of the Son of God; <u>that ye may know that ye have eternal life,</u> and that ye may believe on the name of the Son of God" (1 John 5:13).

In other words, it was important for the saints to know that by receiving Christ, they received God's gift of eternal life. A life which they could live out on a daily basis upon the earth. That means, the earth can experience a new kind of life through the sons of God (or believers in Christ). This is remarkable and worth retaining. *Until we know what we have, we cannot boldly use it.* It is based on such understanding that the Lord Jesus Christ could boldly say of the disciples, **"Ye are the light of the world..."** (Matthew 5:14). Think about that. There was something different about them; His life in them and through them was good enough to light up the world. Halleluiah!

John says, "...*that you may know that you have eternal life...*" Isn't that wonderful? Now that we know that we have this eternal life of God, we are to live from it daily. That is the purpose of knowledge; for use. In other words, those who have received Christ have received eternal life, and can put that to work right away in this present life. It was so important they know that, otherwise they were going to live in hope of what they already had. Imagine having to live through life struggling with things you could deal with, just because you did not know you had the ability. The believer in Christ is living the reality of God's love as stated in John 3:16:

"For God so loved the world, that he gave his only begotten Son, that whosoever believeth in him should not perish, but have everlasting life."

With this knowledge, John 3:16 stirs up thanksgiving towards God. God has already given, and the believer has. Amen. The reason we preach the gospel is so that men may receive what God has given, by believing in His Son Jesus Christ, for in Him is life everlasting; the incorruptible life capable of lighting up the world. It is the life of beauty and excellence, which reveals God's purpose for all things. Halleluiah!

There is no perishing to the believer, because eternal life is indestructible. Nothing can consume or exhaust "eternal" life; nothing on this earth is that big or powerful. Think about that. It means there is nothing in this world which is capable of destroying the believer in Christ. There is no circumstance which can cause the believer to be frustrated, stranded, or defeated. *Eternal life is the generous and unlimited supply of God's very own life or grace in and through a person, causing the person to live and walk as God Himself, revealing God's purpose and love through all things.*

So, the apostle John and Paul said the following in this regard respectively:

"**Ye are of God, little children, and <u>have overcome them:</u> <u>because greater is he that is in you</u>, than he that is in the world**" (1 John 4:4).

"**Nay, in all these things <u>we are more than conquerors</u> through him that loved us**" (Romans 8:37).

What did Paul the apostle know? He knew the beauty of having God's life actively at work in him. He understood what it meant for God to be at work in a man. God is not different from eternal life; He is eternal life. So, to be given eternal life is to be given God Himself. That is the reason the Holy Spirit is given to live in us. He is the communicator or conveyor of the believer's inheritance— *eternal life*— in Christ. That is why Paul the apostle said,

"**But if the Spirit of him that raised up Jesus from the dead dwell in you, <u>he that raised up Christ from the dead shall also</u> <u>quicken your mortal bodies by his Spirit that dwelleth in you</u>**" (Romans 8:11).

You see, the Holy Spirit was responsible for raising Jesus Christ from the dead; He was the communicator of life into the body of Christ. So, Paul the apostle says, that same Spirit, by dwelling in us would also infuse life into our mortal bodies and keep our bodies saturated with life, so that they can neither be corrupted nor destroyed. Halleluiah! The Holy Spirit delights in doing so; He delights in bringing the saints into such rightful participation with their inheritance or calling in Christ. The believer in Christ is a possessor of eternal life by the Spirit in this present world. Think of the seasons and atmospheres that can be associated with such a person; think of what heavenly atmosphere can surround his life.

5. The believer has become an heir of God (son of God) and a joint-heir with Christ

Being made a new creature is actually being made a son of God. The believer in Christ is a son of God because he is born of God by the resurrection of Christ; he is made in the likeness of Christ. That is why Paul the apostle says,

"For it became him, for whom are all things, and by whom are all things, <u>in bringing many sons unto glory</u>, to make the captain of their salvation perfect through sufferings" (Hebrews 2:10).

The coming forth of sons, is the purpose and accomplishment of the resurrection of Jesus Christ; He did not come out of the grave alone; no. He came out with us! Halleluiah! He brought forth sons in the glory of the Father, being a seed of God Himself. The Son of God could only give birth to sons of God. Everything brings forth after its kind. Remember, we had earlier read how the Lord Jesus Christ presented Himself as a seed, saying,

"Verily, verily, I say unto you, Except a corn of wheat fall into the ground and die, it abideth alone: but if it die, it bringeth forth much fruit" (John 12:24).

John 12:24 and Hebrews 2:10 speak of the same thing; many sons to glory and much fruit. In other words, the Lord Jesus Christ was saying, He was a seed that had to be planted (by death), so that by His resurrection (harvest) He would bring many sons to glory. What glory? The glory of the Father. Since everything brings forth after its kind, even so, Christ Jesus, being the Son of God. He was, therefore, the seed of God which brought forth sons of God. That is who a believer is— *a son of God.* This is the greatest accomplishment of Christ upon the earth. To acknowledge our sonship in Christ is to praise the gospel.

So, John says this is great and amazing love; to be born of God and to be His son.

"Behold, what manner of love the Father hath bestowed upon us, <u>that we should be called the sons of God</u>: therefore the world knoweth us not, because it knew him not" (1 John 3:1).

That was why Jesus came. He said,

"But as many as received him, to them gave he <u>power to become the sons of God</u>, even to them that believe on his name…" (John1:12).

By being sons of God, we are equally heirs of God. One cannot be without the other. This is very important to be understood. To say you are a son, you are indirectly saying you are an heir; an heir of your Father. That is who Jesus Christ is; Son of God and Heir of God the Father. So, He said,

"All things are delivered unto me of my Father: and no man knoweth the Son, but the Father; neither knoweth any man the Father, save the Son, and he to whomsoever the Son will reveal him" (Matthew 11:27).

Was it an exaggeration when the Lord Jesus Christ said, *"…all things are delivered unto me of my Father…"*? Certainly not. We know that Christ cannot lie or exaggerate. It is only normal that a son be an heir of all that the Father has. And what did the Father have? LIFE EVERLASTING; His life, which includes His power and glory. Life everlasting speaks of all that God is and owns; that includes the world, to the exclusion of His sovereignty as God. In other words, the son is given all things that the Father is and has, except the Father's sovereign rule as God. We know so because He said,

"For as the Father hath life in himself; <u>so hath he given to the Son to have life in himself</u>; And hath given him authority to execute judgment also, because he is the Son of man" (John 5:26/27).

We see in the verses above that the Father's love for the son has made Him pour out Himself into the son—*life*. In other words, the son became the possessor of all that the Father is. And not only that, but has also given Him the authority to execute judgment; in other words, to decide the outcome of anything. Furthermore, He tells us;

"As thou hast given him power over all flesh, <u>that he should give eternal life</u> to as many as thou hast given him. <u>And this is life eternal, that they might know thee the only true God,</u> and Jesus Christ, whom thou hast sent" (John 17:2/3).

So, as an heir—*being granted all the knowledge of the Father*—He was also responsible for giving that same life (knowledge of the Father) to men. This was to happen by Him sowing Himself as a seed, to "rise up in all men"; even in those that believe. Now, that is the power of an heir; to be given the full knowledge of God by birth in Christ and given the responsibility and power to exercise yourself in the Father's authority. So, believing in Christ or believing the gospel of Christ is receiving your sonship and becoming an heir of God. That is why Paul the apostle could boldly say,

"The Spirit itself beareth witness with our spirit, <u>that we are the children of god</u>: And if children, then heirs; <u>heirs of God, and joint-heirs with Christ</u>; if so be that we suffer with him, that we may be also glorified together" (Romans 8:16/17).

So, in Christ, you are a son of God and an heir of God; a joint-heir with Christ; you are a possessor of all things. Everything that belongs to Christ, belongs to the believer in Christ as well; for all that belongs to God belongs to Christ. Halleluiah! And Christ is proud to share that with us.

6. The believer is given the Holy Spirit

The Holy Spirit is God's promise to all that believe the Gospel. In fact, the Holy Spirit comes to bear witness that we are who and what the gospel says we are, and to begin revealing what our inheritance in Christ is. There is something known as the hope of our calling, which is all that we are called to be and to possess in Christ. So, Paul the apostle prayed that the saints would come to this knowledge saying,

"The eyes of your understanding being enlightened; that ye may know what is <u>the hope of his calling</u>, and what the <u>riches of the glory of his inheritance</u> in the saints," (Ephesians 1:18).

The hope of our calling speaks of the riches of the glory of our inheritance in Christ; it basically speaks of our fellowship (participation) in the Godhead—*in that which the Father shares with the Son.* John speaks of this saying,

"That which we have seen and heard declare we unto you, <u>that ye also may have fellowship with us</u>: and truly <u>our fellowship is with the Father, and with his Son Jesus Christ</u>" (1 John 1:3).

Paul the apostle speaks of this fellowship with the Son, which is an actual participation in and partaking of all that the Lord Jesus Christ is and enjoys with the Father.

"God is faithful, by whom <u>ye were called unto the fellowship of his Son Jesus Christ our Lord</u>" (1 Corinthians 1:9).

This is so important, being the very thought that the Lord Jesus Christ communicated when He said,

"… If a man love me, he will keep my words: and <u>my Father will love him, and we will come unto him, and make our abode with him</u>" (John 14:23).

Paul the apostle also speaks of this inheritance repeatedly in the following verses:

"Giving thanks unto the Father, which hath made us meet to be <u>partakers of the inheritance of the saints in light</u>:" (Colossians 1:12).

"And now, brethren, I commend you to God, and to the word of his grace, which is able to build you up, <u>and to give you an inheritance among all them which are sanctified</u>" (Acts 20:32).

You see, until this is known, the saints cannot consciously walk in the reality of it and in a manner that glorifies God. Knowledge of truth makes free indeed; it matures children into sons in Christ. This is the Father's desire; that we would see ourselves as sons and walk in the reality of that which being a son entails. He wants us to maximize His blessings, and be fruitful in good works to the glory of His name through the fellowship of His Son Jesus Christ. *To bring the saints up to such knowledge of our inheritance and to help us participate in it, is the reason the Holy Spirit is given.*

Paul the apostle beautifully puts it this way:

"In whom also we have obtained an inheritance, being predestinated according to the purpose of him who worketh all things after the counsel of his own will: That we should be to the praise of his glory, who first trusted in Christ. In whom ye also trusted, after that ye heard the word of truth, the gospel of your salvation: in whom also after that ye believed, <u>ye were sealed with that holy Spirit of promise, Which is the earnest of our inheritance until the redemption of the purchased possession,</u> unto the praise of his glory" (Ephesians 1:11-14).

The Holy Spirit basically "helps us" to experience the reality of that which God has said we are and what belongs to us; He brings us into an active participation (fellowship) with Christ and makes manifest in and through us the beauty of the divine life; He is available to teach and to comfort (strengthen and restore) us at all times; the Holy Spirit helps us possess our purchased possession.

Three Major things the Holy Spirit is given for:

1. *The Holy Spirit is given to bear witness in our hearts that we are sons of God and that God is our Father*

"And because ye are sons, <u>God hath sent forth the Spirit of his Son</u> into your hearts, crying, Abba, Father. Wherefore thou art no more a servant, but a son; and if a son, then an heir of God through Christ" (Galatians 4:6/7).

"But when the Comforter is come, whom I will send unto you from the Father, even the Spirit of truth, which proceedeth from the Father, <u>he shall testify of me:</u>" (John 15:26).

2. *The Holy Spirit is given to teach and remind us of the ways of the Lord*

"But the Comforter, which is the Holy Ghost, whom the Father will send in my name, <u>he shall teach you all things, and bring all things to your remembrance,</u> whatsoever I have said unto you" (John 14:26).

"Howbeit when he, the Spirit of truth, is come, <u>he will guide you into all truth:</u> for he shall not speak of himself; but whatsoever he shall hear, that shall he speak: and he will shew you things to come" (John 16:13).

3. *The Holy Spirit is given to bring us into active fellowship with our inheritance (which we have in common) with Christ, including the comfort of the Father*

"Howbeit when he, the Spirit of truth, is come, he will guide you into all truth: for he shall not speak of himself; but whatsoever he shall hear, that shall he speak: and he will shew you things to come. He shall glorify me: <u>for he shall receive of mine, and shall shew it unto you</u>. All things that the Father hath are mine: therefore said I, that he shall take of mine, and shall shew it unto you" (John 16:13-15).

The believer benefits from the ministry of the Holy Spirit who bears witness of Christ, teaches and reminds us of the ways of Christ, and brings the believer into fellowship with the Father and the Son Jesus Christ. That is why the verse we just read says "…*he shall glorify me…*" How would He do that? He told us; "… *he shall receive of mine, and shall shew it unto you…*" That is amazing, because it speaks of helping the believer participate and have the reality of that which Christ Jesus shares with the Father. This is very instrumental as to what becomes of the believer's heavenly atmosphere—*fellowship with the Holy Spirit.*

The Comfort of the Spirit

The Holy Spirit is called The Comforter. The Lord Jesus Christ said,

"But the Comforter, which is the Holy Ghost, whom the Father will send in my name, <u>he shall teach you all things, and bring all things to your remembrance</u>, whatsoever I have said unto you" (John 14:26).

To comfort means to restore, to replace, or cause to recover. That is so important to note. In other words, the Holy Spirit is responsible for creating for us an atmosphere via which anything lost, missing, destroyed, or stolen can be replaced or restored. What a blessing to have the Holy Spirit sent to fulfil such a ministry towards us; He is responsible for the profuse working of eternal life in and through the believer, which is the believer's inheritance. *There is nothing that can happen to a believer beyond the ministry of the Holy Spirit to restore; absolutely nothing.* When we think this way and believe in the ministry of the Holy Spirit, there will be nothing to fear about life and our walk in God's plans and purpose for our lives.

The Holy Spirit replenishes our energy and supplies sufficient resources for us to accomplish the Father's purpose. Remember that the Lord Jesus Christ said one of the things the Holy Spirit will do is to "glorify Him." That is to mean, as He was in person to the disciples, so will the Holy Spirit be in us. The Holy Spirit is given to give to the believer to give him a Psalms 23 experience, *"The Lord is my shepherd, I shall not want"* (Psalms 23:1). The rest of that Psalms lists the benefits of the Holy Spirit, which He does to make verse one stand true. Halleluiah! Verse 3 says, *"...He restores my soul…*" Isn't it wonderful to know that the Holy Spirit restores and refreshes our souls even when we are weary? It is not comfort, unless we are restored according to what is written in God's perfect will in Christ Jesus.

In Isaiah 61:1/3, the Lord Jesus Christ explains His ministry to the saints saying,

"The Spirit of the Lord GOD is upon me; because the LORD hath anointed me to preach good tidings unto the meek; he hath sent me to bind up the brokenhearted, to proclaim liberty to the captives, and the opening of the prison to them that are bound; To proclaim the acceptable year of the LORD, and the day of vengeance of our God; to comfort all that mourn; <u>To appoint unto them that mourn in Zion, to give unto them beauty for ashes, the oil of joy for mourning, the garment of praise for the spirit of heaviness; that they might be called trees of righteousness</u>, the planting of the LORD, that he might be glorified" (Isaiah 61:1-3).

Did you notice, "To comfort all that mourn"? That is the ministry the Holy Spirit also takes upon Himself, because He is sent to represent the exact ministry of the Lord Jesus Christ as a Shepherd to the saints. How does He comfort? *He gives beauty for ashes, He supplies the oil of joy to overcome the sorrow from mourning losses, and He gives a garment of praise to overcome the spirit of heaviness from the burdens of life.* Halleluiah! He says when this is done, then these believers in whom the Holy Spirit is at work will be known as "trees of righteousness." Why would they be called trees of righteousness? Because by the success of the ministry of the Holy Spirit, they would have the experiences of God's good, acceptable, and perfect will; they would be fruitful and prosperous, regardless of the state of affairs in the world. The Holy Spirit was basically responsible for giving the believer the heavenly season. Halleluiah!

Why is this so important to know? It will help you to value the ministry of the Holy Spirit, and the atmosphere He brings into your life; He makes for the unique heavenly atmosphere to those who have received the Lord Jesus Christ via the gospel, and are walking in the light of God's Word.

7. The believer lives in the very presence of God the Father

The Lord Jesus Christ said,

"… I am the way, the truth, and the life: <u>no man cometh unto the Father</u>, but by me" (John 14:6).

Praise the Lord! So, if a person has come to the Father by Christ Jesus, then the person is in the presence of the Father; not as a stranger, but as a son. Such a person has received the presence of the Father as his home. So, we hear the Psalmist say,

"Cast me not away from thy presence; ...." (Psalms 51:11).

You see, the presence of the Father is where the believer lives, and is where the believer must be in order to excel, regardless of the times or seasons of the world. In the old days, the Psalmist said, **"Enter into his gates with thanksgiving, and into his courts with praise: be thankful unto him, and bless his name"** (Psalms100:4). Halleluiah! The believer has entered not to depart anymore; the presence of the Father has become the believer's permanent abode.

So, we hear the Psalmist says,

"Surely goodness and mercy shall follow me all the days of my life: and <u>I will dwell in the house of the LORD for ever</u>" (Psalms 23:6).

You cannot dwell in His house forever and not be in His presence. Halleluiah! So, Paul the apostle says,

"Having therefore, brethren, boldness to enter into the holiest by the blood of Jesus" (Hebrews 10:19).

If the blood has washed away sins and made for the boldness to enter, why will one want to enter and go out? The believer in Christ has come to the Father by Christ, and lives in the presence of the Father. Christ has become the path of life through the gospel to all men. Even as the Psalmist says,

"Thou wilt shew me the path of life: in thy presence is fulness of joy; at thy right hand there are pleasures for evermore" (Psalms 16:11).

If in His presence there is fullness of joy, and at His right hand pleasures for evermore, why will the believer want to be without fullness of joy or without the pleasures of God; which are experiences only possible "in His presence"? That is the reason the Psalmist adds,

"He that dwelleth in the secret place of the most High shall abide under the shadow of the Almighty" (Psalms 91:1).

One has to be in His presence to enjoy the cover of the shadow of the Almighty; that presence of the Lord is the secret place which only those in Christ have been granted access to; it is the believer's safe place. So, it is said,

"The name of the LORD is a strong tower: the righteous runneth into it, and is safe" (Proverbs 18:10).

Of course, it is in the name of Jesus Christ that we find our righteousness, and by this righteousness, we abide in the presence of God the Father. If you are a believer in Christ, God's Word reveals that the presence of the Lord is your dwelling place. And if place decides seasons, and seasons decide atmospheres, then you can know what kind of atmosphere to expect in your life whether asleep or awake. When you understand what it means to be a believer as we have covered in this chapter, then embracing the believer's atmosphere is made easy.

CHAPTER FIVE

THE BELIEVER'S ATMOSPHERE

There exist four major types of atmospheres; the natural atmosphere, the world atmosphere, the human atmosphere, and the heavenly atmosphere. The believer's atmosphere is the heavenly atmosphere; it is greater, higher, and richer than all the other atmospheres. This is one of the main reasons why the Holy Spirit is given to the believer. He brings the believer a foretaste of this heavenly atmosphere, superimposing it over the other atmospheres as need be. It is the atmosphere of the Spirit. This atmosphere is unique to the believer because of the believer's place, which consequently makes for the believer's unique seasons. This unique "place" is the bedrock of the believer's life. Missing out on the believer's place is failing to appreciate the believer's atmosphere.

The Believer's Place

The believer's place is in God. That is where the believer lives, and moves, and has his being; as Paul the apostle said;

"For in him we live, and move, and have our being; …" (Acts 17:28).

If in Him (God), the believer lives, moves, and has his being, then *God is the believer's dwelling place.* So, we hear the Psalmist say,

"Lord, thou hast been our dwelling place in all generations" (Psalms 90:1).

"…thou [God] hast been our dwelling place…" Halleluiah! Think about it. That is why Paul the apostle also said,

"For ye are dead, and your life is hid <u>with Christ in God</u>" (Colossians 3:3).

"…with Christ IN GOD", he says. The believer's life is in God; He is the dwelling place of the believer. This is rightly so because the believer dwells in the very presence of God, made possible by Christ Jesus. He lives in the holy of holies, which the high priests were only able to visit once a year. However, for the believer, this is not just a once a year access, but an eternal dwelling place. Amen. God has offered Himself as the believer's dwelling place. This is what makes for the believer's experience of the kingdom of God, as the Lord Jesus Christ said,

"… Verily, verily, I say unto thee, Except a man be born of water and of the Spirit, <u>he cannot enter into the kingdom of God</u>" (John 3:5).

Today, by the Spirit of God, we are born into God's very own kingdom, in which the believer can have the experience of the heavenly atmosphere. The presence of God covers the territory of His kingdom. It is the air we breathe; God's very own air. It is the life we live; God's very own life. Halleluiah. When the Lord Jesus Christ said,

"…Ye are from beneath; I am from above: ye are of this world; <u>I am not of this world</u>" (John 8:23),

…He spoke of the life in God; He spoke of "the world" of God's kingdom. That is a different place from this world; it is a higher place of absolute power and dominion. While in this world, Jesus Christ lived from that place. It is the same place believers are expected to live from while in this world—*from the heavenly place.* Once again, He spoke of the kingdom being different from this world's, saying,

"Jesus answered, My kingdom is not of this world: if my kingdom were of this world, then would my servants fight,

that I should not be delivered to the Jews: <u>but now is my kingdom not from hence</u>" (John 18:36).

So, there is a kingdom, but not of this world. Paul the apostle admonishes the saints in this wise saying,

"If ye then be risen with Christ, seek those things which are above, <u>where Christ sitteth</u> on the right hand of God. <u>Set your affection on things above</u>, not on things on the earth" (Colossians 3:1/2).

By "where Christ sitteth" and "things above", he was revealing the beauty of the heavenly life which is hid with Christ in God (as told us in verse 2). Remember, we are dealing with the believer's place. Until this is grasped, living boldly in the kingdom would be impossible; causing the believer to be trapped and limited by this present world. So, we hear the Lord Jesus Christ say the same thing about Himself and us not being of this world;

"<u>They are not of the world,</u> even as I am not of the world. Sanctify them through thy truth: thy word is truth. As thou hast sent me into the world, even so have I also sent them into the world" (John 17:16-18).

If the believer is not of this world, then of what world is he of? Certainly, of the world of God's Kingdom; the world of His presence—*the heavenly world*. That is also the world of the Spirit. So, Paul the apostle says,

"If we live in the Spirit, let us also walk in the Spirit" (Galatians 5:25).

The believer's life is IN THE SPIRIT, just as revealed in the verse above. In God, in the Kingdom, and in the Spirit all speak of the same place; where the believer permanently lives or dwells, and ought to walk; "…let us also walk in the Spirit". It is a walk from this place that makes for the believer's atmosphere. *It is only by a walk in the Spirit that the believer's distinction from the world is made known.* Bringing the believer to a unique place in God is what Christ meant when He said,

"In my Father's house are many mansions: if it were not so, I would have told you. I go to prepare a place for you. And if I go and prepare a place for you, I will come again, and receive you unto myself; that where I am, there ye may be also" (John 14:2/3).

By believing in the gospel of Christ (receiving Christ), we come into this prepared place IN GOD, where the Father and Son dwell. This "unique place" is only accessible by the one who has believed the gospel. If you have believed the gospel of the Lord Jesus Christ, then this is your current location—*in God*. From there you will be expected to live.

The Believer and Seasons

Seeing then that the believer has a unique place—*in God, in the Spirit, or in the Kingdom*—the believer therefore also has unique seasons. This is where the main distinction in experiences begins to come forth. Remember, we said place decides what seasons can occur. This reveals that the believer's seasons are not the same as those of the world. And since seasons reveal what activities are expected, you can see why it is required of the believer to have a different kind of priority or lifestyle; his seasons or opportunities are different! That is the reason Paul the apostle said,

"If we live in the Spirit, let us also walk in the Spirit" (Galatians 5:25).

In other words, the believer is to move by the dictates of the seasons of the kingdom (revealed by the heavenly atmosphere), and not by those of this world. And it takes faith to walk according to the seasons of the kingdom; it takes a walk in the light of God's Word. A walk in faith is the standard for a walk in the Spirit, because it opposes the walk in sight which can be influenced by worldly seasons or atmospheres.

"…For we walk by faith, not by sight: …" (2 Corinthians 5:7).

To live by faith (by the Word of God) means to live by what is true in the Spirit (where the believer lives). The Lord Jesus Christ walked by faith; He lived according to Kingdom seasons. When He was asked to go up to the feast, He said,

"…My time is not yet come: but your time is always ready" (John 7:6).

In other words, based on where they were operating from, their standard and His to judge seasons were not the same. Since they were men of sight, to them, the time was right based on their own standards. So, He said, *"… your time is always ready."* But to the Lord Jesus Christ, by virtue of the spiritual season, it was not yet the favourable time for His purpose to be revealed. So, He did not move when they were moving; they moved by world's seasons, but the Lord waited for the heavenly season.

Because the believer's place is different, the believer's seasons are different too. A believer who walks by sight, would very often be out of phase with divine seasons. The Lord Jesus Christ said,

"I can of mine own self do nothing: <u>as I hear, I judge: and my judgment is just</u>; because I seek not mine own will, but the will of the Father which hath sent me" (John 5:30).

Did you see that? There was something He had to observe IN THE FATHER, to know what season was right for what purpose; He had to hear in order to judge justly. He was keen to know the heavenly season. Isaiah the prophet had spoken of how Jesus Christ was to be a man given to Spiritual seasons saying,

"And the spirit of the LORD shall rest upon him, the spirit of wisdom and understanding, the spirit of counsel and might, the spirit of knowledge and of the fear of the LORD; And <u>shall make him of quick understanding in the fear of the LORD: and he shall not judge after the sight of his eyes, neither reprove after the hearing of his ears:</u> But with righteousness shall he judge the poor, and reprove with equity for the meek of the earth: and he shall smite the earth with the rod of his mouth, and with the breath of his lips shall he slay the wicked" (Isaiah 11:2-4).

This is remarkable because a man in God should have good discernment and judgment of the seasons in God. In the case above, Isaiah the prophet spoke of Jesus Christ saying, "**…and he shall not judge after the sight of his eyes, neither reprove after the hearing of his ears: …**" What that means is, He was not going to discern the season using his physical eyes or ears; no! He could tell the right time and the right judgment, without the use of His five senses; "**… WITH RIGHTEOUSNESS shall he judge the poor, and reprove with equity for the meek of the earth…**" This is the reason the Lord Jesus Christ had a different schedule and priority from those of the world; He lived by the seasons of the Spirit. When you understand the believer's seasons, you will have a priority uncommon to the world. *He who dances along with the tune of the world is at variance with the seasons of the kingdom of God.*

The Believer and His Atmosphere

Surely goodness and mercy shall follow me all the days of my life: and <u>I will dwell in the house of the LORD for ever</u> (Psalms 23:6).

Since the believer lives in the presence of the Lord—the house of the LORD, the believer naturally experiences God's seasons and atmosphere. Consequently, "goodness and mercy" is guaranteed to be a part of the believer's life. Halleluiah! Say this to yourself, "*I dwell in the house of the Lord; goodness and mercy follow me all the days of my life.*" Amen. It is important to understand this so the line between the believer's activity in the earth realm and his activity in the Spirit realm can be drawn. Since things happen in the Spirit before they happen in the physical, with physical things mirroring spiritual things, then the believer only walks or reveals on earth that which is already existing in the Spirit. This difference in activity is what makes for the believer's difference in results.

The believer in this world responds based on what has already taken place in the Spirit; he responds by the dictates of the Spirit, and by the light of God's Word. *When spiritual seasons change, the believer is able to identify that by the signs of the spiritual atmosphere, and not by the physical.* So, the believer responds by observing the spiritual atmosphere.

The mind and the Believer's Atmosphere

The believer has to first leave "his place" to suffer or be stranded as the worldly. Wisdom cautions us against leaving our place saying,

"As a bird that wandereth from her nest, so is a man that wandereth from his place" (Proverbs 27:8).

This happens from the soul realm of the believer—*when he allows his soul to be influenced by the happenings in the world than the happenings in the Spirit.* Every man is only safe and flourishes in his place; his place decides his atmosphere. Out of his place, a man is as a wandering birth, at risk of being a prey. Even though by Christ Jesus the believer [in spirit] has been granted access to the Father's presence, it is the responsibility of the believer to renew his mind according to this new environment. That is why the Psalmist says,

"Surely goodness and mercy shall follow me all the days of my life: and I will dwell in the house of the LORD for ever" (Psalms 23:6).

Goodness and mercy only follows because there is "dwelling" in the house of the LORD. From the earth, we stay in our place by renewing our minds. So, Paul the apostle said,

"And be not conformed to this world: but be ye transformed by the renewing of your mind, that ye may prove what is that

good, and acceptable, and perfect, will of God" (Romans 12:2).

The "renewing of the mind" is one of the most critical responsibilities of the believer, which makes for what becomes of the believer's actual atmosphere at any given time. As true and glorious as the believer's atmosphere is in the Spirit, the state of his mind decides how much of that heavenly atmosphere is made manifest. So, Paul cautions the believer to give attention to renewing his mind. He says when that happens, then the believer will have the proofs of God's good, acceptable, and perfect will.

The believer is more likely to deviate from this atmosphere from the mind—soulish realm. The soulish realm is influenced by the five senses. Our five senses are only to be trusted when they are in harmony with God's Word. Otherwise, we are to discard whatever the senses are saying. It takes the Word of God to know whether or not our senses are in harmony with God's. Without the Word of God richly dwelling in us, we will not know what to accept and what to reject. It is the Word of God that gives the believer the life of faith, whereby he exalts the atmosphere of God above that of the world. So, Paul the apostle said,

"…For we walk by faith, not by sight…" (2 Corinthians 5:7).

The reason God's Word instructs us to stay our minds on God, is because God's Word maintains us in His atmosphere. So, it is written,

"Thou wilt keep him in perfect peace, whose mind is stayed on thee: because he trusteth in thee" (Isaiah 26:3).

"Perfect peace"—*the result of the manifestation of the heavenly atmosphere*, happens when the believer's mind is STAYED ON GOD. By so doing, the believer exalts God's thoughts above that of his present unfavourable circumstances. Remember, the believer can only stray off the heavenly atmosphere from his mind. Most times, this is caused by trusting the surrounding circumstances, than trusting the Word of God. When the unfavourable circumstances are trusted, the believer's soul embraces the atmosphere of the world, and will be subjected to defeat.

Casting Down Imaginations

Paul the apostle speaking to the saints on how to deal with their minds, and walk in their divine atmosphere says,

"For the weapons of our warfare are not carnal, but mighty through God to the pulling down of strong holds; Casting down imaginations, and every high thing that exalteth itself against the knowledge of God, and bringing into captivity every thought to the obedience of Christ;" (2 Corinthians 10:4/5).

That is very instructive. There is surely some warring for us to do; it is warring against our imaginations and anything exalting itself above the knowledge of God. Paul the apostle says it is our responsibility to bring the thoughts that come into our minds to the obedience of Christ. When we do this, we simply exalt the heavenly atmosphere, which makes manifest the glory of God. Paul and Silas understood this; they had the option to either sit in prison murmuring and complaining about their situation, or to ascend above it. They chose to ascend above their environment; they became joyful in God by praying and singing praises. In so doing, their atmosphere was synchronized with the heavenly, and miracles began to take place.

Unless the believer ascends above the weight of the issues in this life, he will be trapped in the world's atmosphere and suffer as the ungodly. The Lord said,

"I have said, Ye are gods; and all of you are children of the most High. But ye shall die like men, and fall like one of the princes" (Psalms 82:6/7).

Falling and dying like the ungodly happens when the sons of God fail to put their spiritual wisdom to work. Whenever our hearts become heavy and down casted, it is a sign of a thought, memory, or imagination exalting itself above the good will of God for us. The Psalmist had this experience, and said to his soul,

"Why art thou cast down, O my soul? and why art thou disquieted in me? hope thou in God: for I shall yet praise him for the help of his countenance" (Psalms 42:5).

That is how the Psalmist encouraged himself in the Lord; he said, "*…I shall yet praise him for the help of his countenance.*" That was the way he expressed trust expressed in God and dealt with the depression of his soul. We can speak to our souls this way, and cause it to ascend higher than the sorrow of the time. *A soul that is cast down (broken) does not create an atmosphere of glory.* In fact, wisdom says,

"A merry heart doeth good like a medicine: but a broken spirit drieth the bones" (Proverbs 17:22).

Therefore, if we will experience God's healing or miracle power, we have to keep a joyful heart. He says a joyful heart does good like medicine. On the contrary, a broken spirit (a broken heart or soul) dries up the bones. A sorrowful heart makes things worst.

The Believer's Joyful Atmosphere

Until Jesus returns and completely takes away the cloud of darkness and death over the entire earth, this present life will not give us reasons to be always happy. Of course, that is because of the evil we still have in the world today. Nonetheless, God has not left us as victims to darkness; no. Evil may come, and the unfavourable circumstances may still show up. However, when they do, that is the perfect time to put our spiritual advantages to work as sons of God who have been equipped with the Holy Spirit and with the wisdom of God. While we wait on the return of Christ

Jesus, He has given us the power to rule and reign over darkness (Romans 5:17). It is said,

"Ye are of God, little children, and have overcome them: because greater is he that is in you, than he that is in the world" (1 John 4:4).

Halleluiah! That is who we are; overcomers. We are not to be victims but victors! We have the responsibility to react intelligently in God. We are not to watch the winds of life carry us away, while we sit like people without hope. We do not wait for circumstances to change before we put our spiritual advantages to work; no, we react and intentional maintain our joy in God by trusting His Word. The Bible says,

"Therefore with joy shall ye draw water out of the wells of salvation" (Isaiah 12:3).

In other words, though we have this well of salvation, joy is the secret to benefit (draw) from it. Think about that. Waiting for circumstances to change is putting yourself at the mercy of whatsoever life throws at you. We may not know all the reasons why some unfavourable things happen to us, but God has equipped us and told us how to respond and how to triumph.

The Psalmist tells us of a people, who instead of doing God's Word —*praising, meditating on God, and stirring up their joy,* chose to be sad. They asked,

"How shall we sing the LORD'S song in a strange land?" (Psalms 137:4).

"How shall we sing the LORD'S song in a strange land"? As long as there was no song, there was no joy. No joy meant captivity maintained its dominion, because it was void of the heavenly atmosphere. Paul and Silas, on the other hand, though in a strange land (prison), chose to rise above their surrounding circumstance(s); the Bible tells us,

"...at midnight Paul and Silas prayed, and sang praises unto God: and the prisoners heard them" (Acts 16:25).

While others would have murmured, complained, and let sorrow get the best of them, these men prayed and rejoiced in God. You can read verse 26 to see the miracles that happened because of their joyful atmosphere. These guys did not wait for things to change; no. they provoked it. Praise God! They walked off their current atmosphere of sorrow, and ascended into their heavenly atmosphere in Christ. They saw the glory of the presence of the Lord.

We do not wait to be out of "a strange land" before we sing the Lord's song; no. *It is the Lord's song that brings us out of a strange land*! Paul and Silas rose above their current circumstances; they did not make what they were going through the big deal; they refused to magnify the chains and the prison doors. They magnified the Word of God and rejoiced in God, and the righteous judgment of God was established.

We lose our joy and faint the more, every time we make any unfavourable circumstance our focus. The less joy we have, the less strength we have to deal with the affairs of life. The Bible tells us that Paul and Silas so praised God that the prisoners heard them. In other words, their joy could be told by their song; they changed the atmosphere. Then the miracle:

"... suddenly there was a great earthquake, so that the foundations of the prison were shaken: and immediately all the doors were opened, and everyone's bands were loosed" (Acts 16:26).

Praise the Lord! Our ability to rise above any unfavourable circumstance in this world is fundamental to what becomes of our walk in victory. Believers walk by faith and not by sight. We do not only sing the Lord's song in the land of liberty. In fact, singing the Lord's song in a strange land is the way of faith in God; it is godly wisdom. God's strength is made perfect in our weakness. Rejoicing in God in tough times reveals our trust in God. If "**A merry heart doeth good [like] a medicine: but a broken spirit drieth the bones**" (Proverbs 17:22), and "**...with joy shall ye draw water out of the wells of salvation**" (Isaiah 12:3) are true, then sorrow is the weapon of captivity, destruction, and defeat. Sorrow creates an atmosphere of defeat.

The Bible tells us of Hannah, who was barren. Hannah did not know that the more sorrowful she got, the more frustrating her situation became; sorrow maintained an atmosphere which dried up things, instead of making things flourish. In fact, the Bible clearly tells us that, her adversary (her co-wife) intentionally provoked her because she was barren. Yet Hannah was dearly loved by her husband. It is said,

"...her adversary also provoked her sore, for to make her fret, ..." (1 Samuel 1:6).

Hannah was not able to rise above such an atmosphere; she was often in sorrow. As a result, her bones kept drying up. Hannah did not know how to cast down imaginations and every high thing coming from her adversary, and exalting itself above the knowledge of God. She did not know how to maintain her joy by bringing into captivity these provocative words and thoughts (regarding her circumstance) to the obedience of Christ. Despite all her husband did to make her happy, Hannah was not open to that.

In your life, it is important to celebrate and stick to those who promote your joy, and be careful with those who drain your joy. Hannah struggled to rise above her unfavourable situation and the words of her adversary. But the moment she did, her miracle came forth. The Bible tells us that when she prayed and received the word from Eli the high priest, she **"...went her way, and did eat, and her countenance was no more [sad]"** (1 Samuel 1:18). "NO

MORE SAD" was all Hannah needed; she needed a change in atmosphere! Think about that. As a believer in Christ, you can rise above your current circumstance, and excel in God's good will for your life; you can sing the Lord's song, even in a strange land. We intentionally rejoice in the Lord, regardless. This is how we walk in faith. Habakkuk says,

"Although the fig tree shall not blossom, neither shall fruit be in the vines; the labour of the olive shall fail, and the fields shall yield no meat; the flock shall be cut off from the fold, and there shall be no herd in the stalls: Yet I will rejoice in the LORD, I will joy in the God of my salvation" (Habrews 3:17/18).

"Yet I will rejoice…. I will joy in the God of my salvation" is the language of one whose trust is in God; this is how the believer who has refused to submit to unfavarouble circumstances reacts— *he sings the Lord's song, even in a "strange land."* That atmosphere of joy makes manifest the riches of Christ which brings forth the righteous judgments of God, ruling in favour of the believer. Nehemiah understood the beauty of a joyful atmosphere. He said to the people,

"… Go your way, eat the fat, and drink the sweet, and send portions unto them for whom nothing is prepared: for this day is holy unto our Lord: <u>neither be ye sorry; for the joy of the LORD is your strength</u>" (Nehemiah 8:10).

Halleluiah! He cautioned them about being sorrowful saying, "…*neither be ye sorry, for the joy of the LORD is your strength.*" What an advantage! If they were going to experience God's help or strength, then it was necessary for them to stay joyful in the Lord. Praise God!

On the other hand, the Bible gives us the dreaded consequences of a sorrowful atmosphere saying,

"The vine is dried up, and the fig tree languisheth; the pomegranate tree, the palm tree also, and the apple tree, even all the trees of the field, are withered: <u>because joy is withered away from the sons of men</u>" (Joel 1:12).

That is very cautioning. Everything dried up BECAUSE JOY HAD WITHERED AWAY FROM THE SONS OF MEN. Think about that. You can verify your joy level to tell how dry or flourishing things are for you. The believer's atmosphere promotes the righteousness of God; it is an atmosphere created by trust in God.

The Believer's Activity

The believer's distinction shows forth by his priorities and activities in the world. Isaiah says,

"**If ye be willing and obedient, ye shall eat the good of the land:**" (Isaiah 1:19).

Regardless of the quality of the place and the uniqueness of the season, the activity determines what becomes of the believer's experiences in the world. What the believer makes of seedtime and harvest is what distinguishes the believer. How you respond to God's Word decides the manifestation of the heavenly life and your walk in it. That is the reason Paul the apostle admonishes the saints to walk in the Spirit;

"**If we live in the Spirit, let us also walk in the Spirit**" (Galatians 5:25).

When we talk of the believer's activity, we talk of the believer's walk, which is either sowing to or harvesting of the Spirit. However, to grasp what makes for a believer's activity, it is important that the believer understands what it means to be planted in God, or in the presence of the Lord.

Being planted

To appoint unto them that mourn in Zion, to give unto them beauty for ashes, the oil of joy for mourning, the garment of praise for the spirit of heaviness; <u>that they might be called trees of righteousness, the planting of the LORD, that he might be glorified</u> (Isaiah 61:3).

Something significant is mentioned in the above verse; it says, "*…that they might be called trees of righteousness, THE PLANTING OF THE LORD…*" Then it adds "*…that he might be glorified.*" We know that we glorify the Lord by being fruitful (John 15:8). To glorify means to show forth the beauty and excellence of His purpose by living like Him and having the experiences He designed for us. That is what Peter the apostle says in 1 Peter 2:9;

"But ye are a chosen generation, a royal priesthood, an holy nation, a peculiar people; <u>that ye should shew forth the praises of him</u> who hath called you out of darkness into his marvellous light:"

Fruitfulness is living according to purpose and having God's kind of experiences—the joy of His presence and pleasures at His right hand.

Peter calls that, "showing forth the praises of Him." This is only possible when a person receives beauty for ashes, the oil of joy for mourning, and the garment of praise for the spirit of heaviness. This is what makes for the glory of "the trees" of righteousness, the planting of the Lord by which He is glorified. Amen! The Bible on many occasions refers to men as trees. In this case, the believer is called "a tree of righteousness" because the believer is meant to reveal the glory of God. The phrase worth noting is "the planting of the Lord". That is the condition for the glory to be seen.

Therefore, if you are a tree planted by the Lord, then your life is destined to glorify God.

In the preceding section subtitled, "The believer's place," we saw where the believer's place is – the presence of the Lord. So, in Christ, where is the believer planted? In God's presence. Which we said can also be in His house, in His kingdom, or in the Spirit. *The believer is one planted in the Lord's presence by the Lord Himself.* Because this will be true to the believer, it is written,

"The righteous shall flourish like the palm tree: he shall grow like a cedar in Lebanon. <u>Those that be planted in the house of the LORD</u> shall flourish in the courts of our God" (Psalms 92:12/13).

Once again, we see "*…those that be planted in the house of the LORD…*" Is this a coincidence? No, it is not. Think about this; there is a place where a believer ought to be planted. Only then would the experience of "*…shall flourish…*" come forth. As true as that is in the Spirit, there are the activities from that place that make a difference in the believer's life in the world. Remember, the believer is in the world, but not of the world (John 17:14). And it is worth noting that, it is this glorious difference that will attract persecutions to the believer from the worldly. As a believer in Christ, to walk in God's presence, you must live from His presence.

This is why the Word of God is very important to the believer. The Psalmist says,

"Thy word is a lamp unto my feet, and a light unto my path" (Psalms 119:105).

Did you see what the Word of God is to us? It is for lighting up our feet and path. Why do we need lighted feet and a lighted path? For a walk. The walk is what makes manifest the glory; the walk in the Word is the believer's wisdom for experiencing a glorious life. This is how the believer sets in motion the heavenly atmosphere upon the earth. Remember, the Lord Jesus Christ prayed saying,

"… Thy will be done in earth, as it is in heaven" (Matthew 6:10).

The believer by a walk in the light of God's Word, lives the heavenly life upon the earthly realm. This is very important. This prayer of the Lord was answered by God the Father, and can be lived out by the believer. *By virtue of where the believer is planted, his seasons are always in harmony with God's Word.* That is to mean, walking in the light of God's Word is having the right activity within the heavenly seasons. To get a better understanding of how to walk in the light of God's Word, I will request that you read my book "WHEN GOD LEADS." It provides helpful teachings on hearing God's voice, the different ways God speaks, how to respond to the voice of God, the signs of a God-led life, and a lot more. That book will shed more light on walking within God's seasons, because God never leads out of His presence. And because He does not lead out of His presence, He does not lead out of His seasons.

We see that the Word of God inspires the believer's activities in the Spirit, because the believer is expected to walk in the light of God's Word. Walking in the light of God's Word in the world, is walking in the Spirit. The kind of life the believer lives matter, because the believer's walk will show where he is per time. You do not walk where you are not. That is why God never leads out of His presence. God leads every believer in His presence, which is a walk in God's seasons. Consequently, the believer partakes in God's kind of experiences, regardless of the times and seasons of the world. This is how God gets the believer "planted" in His presence. He does so by His Word.

We can therefore look at a believer's atmosphere to tell what the believer's walk is. By a walk in the Spirit the believer walks in God's seasons, with the atmosphere reflecting that divine season. We see this example practically presented to us in Psalms 1:1-4. Let us explore that a little. With this, we can see how the believer is planted in God by a walk in God's Word.

Verse 1: **Blessed is the man that walketh not in the counsel of the ungodly, nor standeth in the way of sinners, nor sitteth in the seat of the scornful.**

This tells us of what the believer is not supposed to do, because those are the ways (walk) of those who are not living from the presence of God; those are not activities in the light. Such people do not see the path of the Lord (revealed by His Word) in order to know how to walk. Is it possible for a believer to walk in such unrighteous paths of life? Yes; when the ways of the Lord are despised or when the believer is a babe in Christ. (1 Corinthians 3:1). Such unrighteous ways do not reveal the glory of God because they are involved in the wrong activities; they are sowing the wrong seeds and reaping the wrong harvest. So, you see, the believer should neither walk in ungodly counsels, stand in the way of sinners, nor get so comfortable that he sits in the seat of the scornful. That is walking the wrong walk.

Verse 2: **But his delight is in the law of the LORD; and in his law doth he meditate day and night.**

Verse 2 tells us of the believer's activity; the believer's priority. The believer who would experience the glory of a divine atmosphere in the world, is the one whose delight is in God's ways. The amazing thing is that when the believer responds or lives according to God's Word, he dominates every other unfavourable season and causes the glory of God to be revealed. In other words, the ways of God have no regard for worldly seasons. In fact, it even has the ability to dominate the limitations of natural seasons. Whenever God's Word is put to work, what is manifested is the glory of God the Father. Nothing in the world has the ability to withstand nor resist that. The Bible has countless examples of such.

Verse 3: **And he shall be like a tree planted by the rivers of water, that bringeth forth his fruit in his season; his leaf also shall not wither; and whatsoever he doeth shall prosper.**

*Verse 3 begins to explain the experiences (or harvests) of the believer (as a result of respecting verse 2). It now tells us that by virtue of a believer's activities in the Spirit, the believer will have the kind of experiences of a tree planted by the rivers of water. And we know what that place is — the presence of God the Father; it makes the believer flourish at all times, without regard for other seasons nor atmospheres. The believer who walks in the light of God's Word carries a divine atmosphere at all times, because the believer's seasons are always in sync with God's for fruitful works. You see, it says the believer brings forth his fruit in season. An outstanding remark says, "…**his leaf also shall not wither…**" Praise God! And whatsoever he does shall prosper. Why? Because the believer's activities are conditioned by the seasons of the Spirit, guided by the light of God's Word! Isn't that wonderful? By this walk, the believer knows no dryness; it does not exist where he lives and walks.*

Jeremiah emphasizes the same flourishing life of the believer by a walk in the Spirit saying,

"For <u>he shall be as a tree planted by the waters</u>, and that spreadeth out her roots by the river, and shall not see when

heat cometh, but her leaf shall be green; and shall not be careful in the year of drought, neither shall cease from yielding fruit" (Jeremiah 17:8).

"He shall be as a tree planted by the waters." That is the same thought communicated in verse 3 of Psalms 1. Who is this man? What kind of a man is he? Verse 7 of Jeremiah 17 tells us;

"Blessed is the man that trusteth in the LORD, and whose hope the LORD is."

That tells us trust is an activity by the Word of God; it is a walk in God's ways. Verse 8 of Jeremiah 17 says this person who lives by God's Word is one **"…that spreadeth out her roots by the river, and shall not see when heat cometh, but her leaf shall be green; and shall not be careful in the year of drought, neither shall cease from yielding fruit."** Isn't it just so wonderful to know what the experiences of the believer are? What distinction! What flourishing with disregard for the times of the world! Look at this; *"…her leaf shall be green…"* Amen. Even more, *"…and shall not see when heat cometh."* It means the believer walking in the light of God's Word is not subject to natural seasons (because some natural seasons in the world have been corrupted by human activities), neither will the believer be careful (worried) in the year of drought! Praise the Lord! So, there will be drought to those living and walking in a place other than in the Spirit. To the believer it says, "...**neither shall [the believer] cease from yielding fruit.**" Halleluiah!

Why will this believer not cease to yield fruit? The believer will continually bear fruit because of "the place"; he is living in the presence of the Lord, and is planted by the river-side. So, there is no point in time where the believer is out of a flourishing season of life; never! It is therefore not possible for such a person to be barren or unfruitful! Everything about the life and walk of the believer evolves within divine life; dryness does not exist there.

Thou wilt shew me the <u>path of life:</u> in thy presence is fulness of joy; at thy right hand there are pleasures for evermore (Psalms 16:11).

Again,

"But <u>the path</u> of the just is as the shining light, that shineth more and more unto the perfect day" (Proverbs 4:18).

The path of the believer is the path of life. By walking therein, he shines more and more unto the perfect day. Isaiah puts it this way,

"...he will teach us of his ways, and we will walk in his paths: for out of Zion shall go forth the law, and the word of the LORD from Jerusalem" (Isaiah 2:3).

Be mindful of the fact that paths are for walk. The Word reveals the path. And the walk in the path makes for the unique and fruitful

experiences for the believer.

Being in the Spirit and not walking in the Spirit will not amount to much. We saw earlier that the seasons of the world can be corrupted. The reason it happens so is because human activities upon the earth can decide the frequency of natural seasons. *If humans live out of season or in abuse of seasons, they decide what becomes of their frequency; seasons can delay or come sooner than expected, based on human activity upon the earth.* That will certainly not be in favour of the earth or humans. It is the reason why the believer who is planted in God's presence is made to partake of God's seasons which are pure and accurate; they can never be corrupted or fail. It is the reason the believer has no respect for drought in the world and cannot cease being fruitful. *If we do not share the same seasons, we cannot have the same results.* That is a fact.

The Lord Jesus Christ gave us this lesson when He said,

"Lay not up for yourselves treasures upon earth, where moth and rust doth corrupt, and where thieves break through and steal..." (Matthew 6:19).

In other words, the things in the world are not sure; they cannot be trusted because they can and have been tampered with by man. Consequently, they cannot sustain or provide adequate beauty for life as they were designed to. That is the purpose for the sons of God now on earth as revealed in Romans 8:19-21. It reads;

"For the earnest expectation of the creature waiteth for the manifestation of the sons of God." For the creature was made subject to vanity, not willingly, but by reason of him who hath subjected the same in hope, Because the creature itself also shall be delivered from the bondage of corruption into the glorious liberty of the children of God."

You see, even creation knows that it has been subjected to bondage; it has been corrupted and cannot perform as it is supposed to. We also know that this is the result of corrupt men upon the earth, who are void of divine understanding; men who have not acknowledged the righteousness and sovereignty of Christ Jesus—*the Word of God*. Therefore, their activities have corrupted creation, and made it unfaithful to its original purpose in God. Meanwhile, creation is waiting for the sons of God in order to be free and to be restored to its original glorious purpose in God.

This is the reason why the believer cannot be left to the corruptible seasons of men; for they will resist the goodness of God and keep it from showing forth in the life of believers – *the sons of God*. That is why God has planted them in Himself, so that from Him they can live beyond the corruption in the world. Only then can God release this river of living water (river of life), causing "the trees" – *the sons of God to flourish,* whose leaves will be for the healing of the nations; even for the redemption of corrupt creation into the same liberty of the sons of God (See Revelation 22:1/2).

In regard then of the present corrupt state of man and the world, the Lord requested that the believer should not lay up his treasure here on earth. In other words, do not place your trust on the unstable and unfaithful things of this present world, for they are surely going to disappoint. He says, for the world is a place **"…where moth and rust doth corrupt, and where thieves break through and steal:** (Matthew 6:19).

This is how unstable, unsure, and unfaithful the people, things, places, and even the seasons of this world can be. They are not to be trusted; you are not to carry out your activities by their dictates, knowledge, or ways, because they surely are not true. What the Lord Jesus Christ is saying is that, to trust in them is to be disappointed, because they will not return to you according to your investment. Your investments will be corrupted by rust; they will be caused to change their form or lose their integrity, and others may be stolen. He only said that to give us wisdom on what to do, saying,

"But lay up for yourselves treasures in heaven, where neither moth nor rust doth corrupt, and where thieves do not break through nor steal: For where your treasure is, there will your heart be also" (Matthew 6:20/21).

What does He mean? The Lord is asking us to live from the Spirit and walk in the Spirit; the believer is to let God's Word be the guide for his activities. In that realm—*the realm of the Spirit,* there is no corruption, and there are no thieves; everyone and everything maintains its integrity according to the praise of God. From there, the believer rules the world because the kingdom of God is faithful; it is higher than this present world. That is why the Word of the Lord through Jeremiah says,

"Thus saith the LORD; <u>Cursed be the man that trusteth in man, and maketh flesh his arm, and whose heart departeth from the LORD. For he shall be like the heath in the desert,</u> and shall not see when good cometh; but shall inhabit the parched places in the wilderness, in a salt land and not inhabited" (Jeremiah 17:5/6).

We are taught by the verses above that a dry plant is one planted in the desert—*in the corrupt world*; it is one which does not live by the light of God's Word. This is a man who has placed his trust in the "arm of flesh" which is corruptible. The Bible says this man is cursed already. That tells us how blessed or curse a man is, is fundamentally decided by his trust, because his trust tells his priorities and activities; these tell a man's path—*where he walks*. It says such a person's heart has departed from the Lord.

Verse 4: **The ungodly are not so: but are like the chaff which the wind driveth away.**

The ungodly do not have a flourishing experience, because they have different priorities, based on the way of life they have. Verse 4 says they are not as the godly; they are unstable and carried about like the chaff which "the wind" (the challenges of life) drives away.

We see how important it is for the believer to walk in the Spirit, for only then will the experiences of the believer be different from those of the world and consistent with God's perfect will. That is why the Lord Jesus Christ said, **"If ye know these things, happy are ye if ye do them"** (John 13:17). It is in doing (walking in the paths of life), that the believer's beautiful experiences are decided or created. In God, the believer's season is always right, and made useful or profitable by a walk in the light of God's Word – *a walk in the Spirit.*

The Believer and His Experiences

The state of the season decides the atmosphere; and the atmosphere reveals the state of the season.

The activity of the believer within a given season creates the believer's atmosphere. The created atmosphere is proof of the state of the season, which also decides what activities are expected or can take place within that season. The first season would be one for the activity of sowing, and the second season would be one for the activity of harvest. Harvest speaks of the believer's experiences. *If you are sensitive to walk in the seasons of the Spirit, not only would you have activities within these seasons, but you too (being a place) will have seasons with atmospheres, which attract or resist certain activities.* Attracted or resisted activities will make for what becomes of the believer's experiences. Presence or absence will always make for an experience. You feel different based on what you have and what you do not have. Both are states which make for a man's experience. *You see, the state of a season (by a given activity) decides atmosphere. And atmosphere reveals what activities are required on that field.*

So, earlier we saw what the Lord Jesus Christ said,

"Hereafter I will not talk much with you: for <u>the prince of this world cometh, and hath nothing in me</u>" (John 14:30).

The question is, what would have happened if the prince of this world had something in Jesus? You see, we just said the state of the field would make for the atmosphere. The atmosphere decides attraction and resistance, and what activities can take place on that field. So, if we say Jesus Christ is a place, then the prince of this world needed that "place" (Christ)to be seasonal (or consistent) with his activities without which, he was not going to be able to exercise authority over Christ. Remember, the dark places of the earth are full of the habitations of cruelty. But we know that Jesus Christ said of Himself, **"...I am the light of the world"** (John 9:5). That is the reason the Lord Jesus said "...*has nothing in me.*" That was to say there was neither room, opportunity, nor consistency for his works to stand. Praise the Lord; the activity of cruelty which Satan works out could not be planted in Christ. We spoke earlier of the beauty of forgiveness. Paul the apostle says,

"Be ye angry, and sin not: let not the sun go down upon your wrath: Neither <u>give place to the devil</u>" (Ephesians 4:26/27).

It is therefore possible to give the devil place! To give him place means to have something of his in you, or to have something in you that makes you consistent with his seasons of activity. It can be unforgiveness, lust, jealousy, sorrow, evil thinking, etc. These things make a person's seasons consistent with the devil's works. And if you are consistent with his seasons, he will tell by the quality or composition of your atmosphere. That atmosphere in itself is a message which tells everyone what you are ready for. In the case above, Paul the apostle says letting the sun go down on your wrath is to give place to the devil.

We see Paul the apostle admonishing the saints on how to be in sync with God's own seasons saying,

"Finally, brethren, whatsoever things are true, whatsoever things are honest, whatsoever things are just, whatsoever things are pure, whatsoever things are lovely, whatsoever things are of good report; if there be any virtue, and if there be any praise, think on these things" (Philippians 4:8).

He gave them something to think about, because it was important what thoughts they had in mind. *These thoughts decide the state of a man's life; they are the activities by which a man seeds his cloud and influences his seasons in the Spirit. This consequently creates a man's atmosphere, and decides what he attracts or resists.* It was imperative that believers understood that, if they were going to maintain their divine seasons and atmospheres in this present world, they had to take control of their thoughts, and think in alignment with God's righteousness and seasons. The believer's atmosphere has to be consistent with the good things that the Lord has planned for His children, so that they can have the right experiences of God's good will. Remember, He said,

"For I know the thoughts that I think toward you, saith the LORD, thoughts of peace, and not of evil, to give you an expected end" (Jeremiah 29:11).

When this atmosphere is right, then the interventions of the Spirit are justified. Even angels can smoothly minister to and for the saints, given that their atmosphere points to the readiness of the saint's season for ceaseless fruitfulness and a reflection of the glory of the Lord. By maintaining activity in the Spirit, the saint sows seeds which creates a certain experience to the glory of God the Father. So, whatever glorifies the Father indeed becomes the saint's experience. Remember, *God only leads in the path of His presence.* His presence being the root of the believer's experiences.

We see the beautiful example of the three Hebrew boys; Shadrach, Meshach, and Abednego. They lived a life in obedience to God's Word; they were walking in the Spirit. Their seasons and activities were consistent with God's. Because God leads in the path of His presence, no man could impose a new place, season, or atmosphere on them. The presence of the Lord was always right there with them. You see, *where we walk reveals where we are.* We are told that the mighty men who took them into the fire were consumed by the very fire, whereas these believers were not. (Daniel 3:22). What was different between the men who were burnt by the fire and these Hebrew believers who were not? Place! Their place decided presence, and presence made the difference.

The fourth man (Christ—*the presence of the Lord*) did not just show up in the fire; no; He was not waiting for the fire; He was with them all the way because they walked in the path of God's presence. If He showed up only in the fire, then they ought to have been burnt by the fire like the mighty men who carried them into the furnace. But that was not the case, because they walked all along in the presence of the Lord; they and the mighty men were in two different places; one in the presence of the Lord and the other in the world. *Challenges only make "the fourth man" visible in the believer's life, though He is there all the time.* What a faithful God! Remember: "**...Lord, thou has been our dwelling place...**"

Atmosphere reveals presence just as atmosphere decides presence. Atmosphere can be a consequence and it can be a cause. Someone can carry his atmosphere into a place and change the atmosphere of others (See subsection of Chapter 1; Atmosphere and Influence). *Atmosphere decides preservation or destruction; atmosphere decides our emotion.* As long as the earth remains, "**...cold and heat...**" (atmosphere), shall not cease. It is said, "**...righteousness, peace, and joy in the holy ghost**" (Romans 14:17).

Remember, atmosphere can be perceived, naturally and spiritually. So, in the case of the three Hebrew boys, the presence of the Lord made for their season, and their season made for their atmosphere. They were preserved by the Lord's atmosphere around them. It is worth noting, that the presence of the Lord decides the believer's atmosphere, and atmosphere decides preservation or destruction. Why did the fire have no effect over Shadrach, Meshach, and Abednego? Because they were in the presence of the Lord; not only in the fire, but also prior to the fire. The fire only made His presence visible. *Challenges reveal the beauty of God in the life of the believer.*

The King said,

"… Lo, I see four men loose, walking in the midst of the fire, and they have no hurt; and the form of the fourth is like the Son of God" (Daniel 3:25).

Because these guys were completely separate from the natural place and atmosphere, their testimony reads:

"And the princes, governors, and captains, and the king's counsellors, being gathered together, saw these men, upon whose bodies the fire had no power, nor was an hair of their head singed, neither were their coats changed, nor the smell of fire had passed on them" (Daniel 3:27).

This is the kind of testimony or praise report God wants His children to have before the world. Such testimonies make the world believe that truly, we are in this world but not of the world. The fire had no power on their bodies; their hair was not singed, neither did their clothes change, nor did they even smell of the smoke therein. These men were completely saturated by God's own atmosphere; the very presence of the Lord that protected and preserved them from destruction. Halleluiah! Do you see the beauty in laying up your treasure in heaven or in walking in God's paths? This is similar to the testimony of the Lord regarding the Israelites; the Lord testified of the blessedness of their lives saying,

"… I have led you forty years in the wilderness: your clothes are not waxen old upon you, and thy shoe is not waxen old upon thy foot" (Deuteronomy 29:5).

Isn't that wonderful? Even the sun did not have enough power to wax old their clothes, nor the ground strong enough to wax old their shoes! Think about that; the glory of the Lord (not the experiences of the world) was the preserving power of these saints. It is worth noting that God does not make promises based on human integrity, but based on His integrity as God. In other words, His commitment to do what He says He will do stands sure, regardless of the state of affairs of the seasons of the world; God will do what He says He will do, as long as there is the believer to walk in the Spirit. God's faithfulness is good for all seasons; it stands true for all times. He will do what He says He will do, not according to the excellence of the health-care system in the world, the economy, nor according to natural or human seasons; no. He performs His Word according to His riches in glory by Christ Jesus. It has no respect for any of these seasons, but for the name of the Lord. Halleluiah.

When Paul the apostle promised the believers that their needs would be supplied by God, he was not saying so in regard of how well the times will turn out or how well the systems of the world would favour them; no. God was not going to be limited by the systems or corruption in the world to get His Word done. So, Paul said,

"…my God shall supply all your need <u>according to his riches in glory by Christ Jesus</u>" (Philippians 4:19).

Praise the Lord! The riches of God by Christ Jesus were to ensure that the saints lacked nothing, because they walked in the Spirit and had their activities therein. Their experiences were not given to same conditions as those of the worldly or unbelieving. Their supply was not decided by the seasons of man or of the world, but by God's seasons—*where they sowed.* If you sowed to the world, expect your harvest from the world; expect that it to be corrupted or to fail; expect that things to change for you according to the changing world and changing times.

A lot of factors prevent the world from being true and pure for the wellbeing of man. But if you sow to the Spirit, then OF THE

SPIRIT should you expect your harvest (not of this world). In other words, if you have your activity in the Spirit, you will of the Spirit have the kind of satisfying experience which cannot be limited by this world and its affairs; you will be supplied from the well of God's unlimited resources—*life everlasting*. It is very important to understand the depths of the Spirit, even of eternal life in Christ, to truly maximize the purpose. John the apostle said,

"These things have I written unto you that believe on the name of the Son of God; <u>that ye may know that ye have eternal life</u>, and that ye may believe on the name of the Son of God" (1 John 5:13).

As true as that is, eternal life is only profitable in this present life by the believer's walk in the Spirit. So, understanding eternal life is important for a walk in it. God the Father supplies or takes care of the believer from the wealth of the riches of glory by Christ Jesus; that is what is called life everlasting; even as used here by Paul the apostle:

"For he that soweth to his flesh shall of the flesh reap corruption; but he that soweth to the Spirit shall of the Spirit reap life everlasting" (Galatians 6:8).

That is the same thought the Lord Jesus Christ spoke of, when he told us not to lay up for ourselves treasures upon the earth, which are corruptible. A believer can choose what to trust by how he lives—*by the priorities he sets in life*. Paul the apostle says, man would reap whatever he chooses to sow. Isn't that cautioning enough? It certainly is. So, his advice was that the believer should sow to the Spirit, and of the Spirit reap life everlasting. *This life everlasting, is the glory of the Father over the believer, setting the believer apart from the light of the world (which is up one moment, and down another).* To depend on the light of the sun would mean to be trapped by the corruptible understanding and ways of the world, which decide an unfavourable experience for humans. So, Isaiah the prophet speaking along this line says,

"**The sun shall be no more thy light by day; neither for brightness shall the moon give light unto thee: <u>but the LORD shall be unto thee an everlasting light, and thy God thy glory.</u> Thy sun shall no more go down; neither shall thy moon withdraw itself: <u>for the LORD shall be thine everlasting light, and the days of thy mourning shall be ended</u>**" (Isaiah 60:19/20).

Twice it is said, "...*for the LORD shall be thine everlasting light...*" Prior to that, it lets us know what would not be required to decide what becomes of our experiences. It says, "**The sun shall be no more thy light by day; neither for brightness shall the moon give light unto thee:**" Praise God we would not have to depend on "these corruptible things", which can be influenced by man; blessed be God, He is our everlasting light and our glory. What that means is the believer is never to walk in darkness, for there will not be a time of lights out for the believer.

Think about that; as the Lord lives on, so the fruitfulness of the believer. Amen. That is what Paul the apostle was referring to as sowing to the Spirit; that the believer will reap "life everlasting." It is the believer's inexhaustible well, and a sure source which is not limited by human times and seasons. Praise the Lord! The believer's season makes for the believer's atmosphere which results in glorious experiences unique to the sons of God; it is the way the sons of God live the answered prayers of Christ, "Thy will be done

CHAPTER SIX

MASTERING YOUR ATMOSPHERE

One thing is needful

Every Atmosphere has a fragrance or a savour; it is either attracting or repelling someone or something. We cannot pray for every one of our needs, neither can we work for every one of them. The responsibility to mind every detail of life is not given to man. Life is too great and too complicated to be managed exclusively managed by our conscious human intelligence. There is a more excellent way to go about life. As much as prayer is vital to man, it is not meant for man to list all of his needs before God. In fact, the Lord Jesus Christ made us to understand that it is not required of us to do so.

But when ye pray, use not vain repetitions, as the heathen do: for they think that they shall be heard for their much speaking (Matthew 6:7).

He was not by that saying we should not persist on some particular changes we may want to see take place, but that we should not take prayer as what we must to do to have all of our needs met, as though if we failed to mention all of what we needed, God would forget to do them. And by the way, how many of your needs are you really aware of? There is a lot about our lives that we neither aware of, nor know how to go about. The Lord went further to say,

"Be not ye therefore like unto them: for your Father knoweth what things ye have need of, before ye ask him" (Matthew 6:8).

He meant good and acceptable prayer is not about much talking (it is not dependent on the number of needs you have mentioned). We surely cannot name everything at prayer, especially when praying with our understanding. Does that mean God will not do that which was not mentioned? Certainly not. We must therefore be careful not to be like the heathen or act like them. He says for our Father knows THE THINGS we have need of, even before we ask. Think about that! Imagine that every time you came to God in prayer, you came with a mindset settled on the fact that God is already aware of the things you need. If we are therefore not to come as though prayer is meant to list our needs, then there must be a better way through which God meets all our needs. *That would mean prayer is not only about asking, but it is more about submitting to God to receive what He already knows we need, and has already made provision for in His love.* Halleluiah!

It is important to understand that, so you can move your attention to focus on what God expects of you. *There is always the one thing we can do which gets all of our needs met. Those who give attention to the one needful thing will not have to manage or care about every other thing.* The Gentiles are different because their priorities are at variance with God's "one thing" that is needful; they have no consciousness and no understanding of God as Father (source and sustainer). Consequently, they tend to manage the details of their lives. Which is tedious and burdensome responsibility, not given to any human.

That is what makes them busy (disregarding God) and burdened by life. This is not God's restful way for His children. Do you remember Martha? She was busy with many things when Jesus visited their home; she was just as overwhelmed by the many burdens of life as the heathens are. Martha was not conscious of the restful life in God that required that we do just the one thing that is needful. So, the Lord corrected her by saying,

"... Martha, Martha, thou art careful and troubled about many things: But <u>one thing is needful</u>: and Mary hath chosen that good part, which shall not be taken away from her" (Luke 10:41/42).

We can either give ourselves to the one thing that is needful or be careful and troubled about every other thing. *Mastering the believer's atmosphere would require that the believer focuses on the one thing, believing that it will address every other thing.* Will you believe "the one thing" God will like you to stick to? Will you choose God's wisdom over yours? We can always choose to either go after the flies or go after the meat. Which do you think is more restful? Going after the rotten meat of course; that will indirectly address the flies. While it is true that chasing the flies may eventually get them to leave after much effort, expect them to return again (sooner or later) as long as the rotten meat remains. *To ignore the one thing that is needful is to be busy after every other thing.* That will result in life being wearisome and eventually frustrating. "One thing is needful", the Lord said to Martha. How willing are you to treat such words seriously? If we master this one thing, then we will find rest in the Lord. So, He said,

"Therefore take no thought, saying, What shall we eat? or, What shall we drink? or, Wherewithal shall we be clothed? (For after all these things do the Gentiles seek:) for your heavenly Father knoweth that ye have need of all these things. But seek ye first the kingdom of God, and his

righteousness; and all these things shall be added unto you" (Matthew 6:31-33).

That is very similar to the advice given to Martha. While every other thing may be vying for your attention, choose the one thing that matters, and every other thing will take care of itself! *When first things come first, second things cease to be a concern or a burden; they take care of themselves.* A wise person knows what first thing or what one thing addresses the rest; and he goes for it. All Paul and Silas did was pray and sing praises, then the gates and the chains gave way of their own accord. It was much easier to deal with the chains and the Roman prison doors, when first things came first. Imagine what it would do for you today, if you would only make first things your priority.

Creation Honours Order

When God's Word—His way, becomes our focus, His glory becomes our effortless testimony.

All creation has intelligence; it knows how to respond to the man giving attention to the one thing that is needful, and it knows how to disregard those despising first things. In other words, the one thing necessary is superior to the others, and commands them to align. The three Hebrew boys in Babylon under the reign of King Nebuchadnezzar did not pray about the fire; no. All they did was obey the Lord, and the fire knew how to behave itself. Obeying the Lord was the first thing, the fire was the second; the latter behaved itself.

All Daniel did was obey the Lord, and he had no energy to waste fighting the lions in the Den; the lions knew how to respect those who put first things first. *Creation is made to follow after man; it honours the man who is after godliness, and dishonours the man who has no regard for godliness. Creation only gets corrupted by human disorder—the despise of God. Putting first things first reveals the fear of God, the dignity in divine protocol, and releases an aroma of divine beauty and authority. The universe can perceive this aroma.*

Instead of going after the ants one after another, why not just go for the sugar? Sometimes, our many worries in life are the results of not minding the one needful thing. Our numerous troubles most often than not, reveal our disobedience or rebellion to God's "one needful thing." God calls us into rest by giving us the one necessary thing to do, which takes care of every other thing. So, the Lord Jesus Christ said,

"...seek ye first the kingdom of God, and his righteousness; **and all these things shall be added unto you**" (Matthew 6:33).

In other words, all the things you could waste your time, energy, and resources going after are covered in one—*the kingdom and the righteousness therein*. If we take the kingdom to heart, then the world and circumstances will submit to us. Why would someone believe this and choose to run after every other thing? The kingdom is God's priority; His righteousness should be all we care about. That is the call of the sons of God, and that is what makes for their manifestation in glory. To live the kingdom life is to live the restful life.

Now in Christ, we have received the Kingdom; we are in a different place. What you need to do after knowing this is to embrace the kingdom life as priority; not that of the world. That is the one thing the believer has to do, as revealed by the Word of God. That is why the Lord Jesus commended Mary by saying,

"**...Mary hath chosen that good part, which shall not be taken away from her.**"

And again,

"Take my yoke upon you, and learn of me; for I am meek and lowly in heart: and <u>ye shall find rest unto your souls</u>. For my yoke is easy, and my burden is light" (Matthew 11:29/30).

Why would you know this and choose the burdensome way of life, when your soul can find rest? Why would you know that there is a yoke which is easy and a burden which is light, and still prefer to go for something tougher, weightier, more wearisome? Mastering your atmosphere is mastering the atmosphere of the Kingdom; it is the atmosphere of the divine life in Christ. It is consciously living on earth from the consciousness of where you are in the spirit— *the heavenly places in Christ.* That is why Paul the apostle said,

"If we live in the Spirit, let us also walk in the Spirit" (Galatians 5:25).

The walk in the Spirit is what makes for the believer's atmosphere because by so doing, the believer is maximizing "the place"—*the Father's presence and seasons of the Spirit.* They are ever favourable for the manifestation of God's glory. The blessed man is the man living by the Word; he is the one whose heart has embraced God's kingdom and His righteousness. This is the man who is like a tree planted by the rivers of water (Psalms 1:3). The light of God's

Word is what shows us how to walk in the Spirit and constantly have the right atmosphere.

Thy word is a lamp unto my feet, and a light unto my path (Psalms 119:105).

Paths are meant for walking, and walking is an activity which seeds and creates a harvest. This is a walk in the path of life, even as revealed by the Word of God (Psalms 16:11). *The believer's atmosphere on earth is a harvest of spiritual activities in the Word.* Whenever we live the Word or do the Word, we influence our atmosphere and make it consistent with that which is true in the Spirit. By that atmosphere comes all that is necessary for our wellbeing and flourishing.

But thou, O LORD, art a shield for me; my glory, and the lifter up of mine head (Psalms 3:3).

You see, if the Lord is the believer's shield and glory, then the glory of the Lord makes for the believer's atmosphere. So, the believer who would master his atmosphere needs to master the glory of the Lord, which is generated by a walk in the light of God's Word.

And the LORD will create upon every dwelling place of mount Zion, and upon her assemblies, a cloud and smoke by

day, and the shining of a flaming fire by night: <u>for upon all the glory shall be a defence</u> (Isaiah 4:5).

Staying Attractive to God

And there came a voice from heaven, saying, Thou art my beloved Son, <u>in whom I am well pleased</u> (Mark 1:11).

The person who takes pleasure in you matters when it comes to living out your purpose. *When you become man's delight, you attract man's favour; but when you become God's delight, you attract God's favour.* That is how the Lord Jesus Christ lived; both God and men took delight in Him.

And Jesus increased in wisdom and stature, and in favour with God and man. (Luke 2:52).

As we have seen in previous sections, favour does not just happen; it is not a product of chance; no. People or things cannot be attracted to you without reason. The Lord Jesus Christ increased in wisdom and in stature, and consequently, He increased in favour. Both God and men increasingly delighted in Him. Something about Christ secured the graciousness of God towards

Him. The sun rises over all the earth but shines best on those who position themselves under it. Those who position themselves under the sun declare that they love the sun. Consequently, the sun loves them in return. The Lord Jesus Christ said,

"And he that sent me is with me: the Father hath not left me alone; for I do always those things that please him" (John 8:29).

It is not enough for men to delight in you; God has to take delight in who you are as well and be pleasured by who you are. Man's delight can be limited to what his senses can perceive; but divine delight is beyond the natural senses. In fact, divine delight is first interested in the heart of a man, then his works.

This is what happened to Samuel when he was sent by God to anoint David as king over Israel. God saw a delightful or pleasurable quality in David which no one else saw or could identify; not even Samuel the prophet.

And it came to pass, when they were come, that he looked on Eliab, and said, Surely the LORD'S anointed is before him. But the LORD said unto Samuel, Look not on his countenance, or on the height of his stature; because I have refused him: for the LORD seeth not as man seeth; for man

<u>looketh on the outward appearance, but the LORD looketh on the heart</u> (1 Samuel 16: 6-7).

In the above verses, we see the limitation of man's sight which can greatly influence his judgement. Eliab in the sight of Samuel the prophet was the most favourable candidate; probably because of the beauty of his countenance or stature. That was good enough to attract Samuel's attention as a man. But God said, "…*the LORD seeth not as man seeth; for man looketh on the outward appearance, but the LORD looketh at THE HEART (the mind).*"

Who you are and what you have in your mind is what fundamentally influences your walk in divine favour. How do you see yourself? What thoughts do you have in mind concerning others or even yourself? *There is an aroma that emanates from every thought; every thought carries or attracts a presence or a personality.* A thought is deciding your favour or disregard. A man is first of his heart before he is of his works. The Lord Jesus Christ said, "**…for out of the abundance of the heart the mouth speaketh**" (Matthew 12:34).

God did not say "…. this is my beloved Son in whom I am well pleased…" because Jesus Christ did something, but because of who He was in his heart or in His mind; it was because of the delight of His heart to obey and fulfil the Father's will. He was inclined to pleasing God the Father by doing His will. So, He said to us,

"Take my yoke upon you, and learn of me; for <u>I am meek and lowly in heart:</u> and ye shall find rest unto your souls" (Matthew 11:29).

The quality of a man's mind and the flavour generated by his thoughts, are deciding the quality of his favour.

While your heart will influence divine resonation or approval toward you, your works (which come from your heart) will influence man's favour towards you. God judges by the aroma of a man's heart, but men judge by the aroma perceived by the senses. *Something you are or have, something men can see, taste, smell, feel, and hear, is deciding the favour of men toward you.*

It is said the Lord Jesus Christ grew in favour both with God and with men. In other words, he was able to live a life delightful to God (by virtue of his heart) and to men (by virtue of his acts). Because God sees the heart before the act, a man enjoys favour first with God before with men. Notice that it is said, He grew in favour with God (first), then with men (second).

It is the approved state of a man's heart towards God, that makes for His approved standard of life towards men.

We are Made for Praise

But thou art holy, O thou that inhabitest the praises of Israel (Psalms 22:3).

Praise is the revelation of the excellence, glory, or standard of God's purpose. Anything functioning within its purpose is praising God. Whenever we "make known" or emphasize the purpose of God, God is praised. So, it is said,

"But ye are a chosen generation, a royal priesthood, an holy nation, a peculiar people; that <u>ye should shew forth the praises of him</u> who hath called you out of darkness into his marvellous light:" (1 Peter 2:9).

The underlined statement says our lives are to show forth God's praises. In other words, we are to reveal the essence of our being by expressing the purpose for which God made us. *Anytime we are functioning according to purpose— revealing the excellence of God's glory, we are making known God's praises.* This can occur by the quality of our thoughts, words, or actions. Any activity that we carry out, within God's divine purpose makes known the savour of His purpose—*praise*. Psalms 22:3 which we read earlier, says God "… *inhabits the praises of Israel.*" That is why the Lord Jesus Christ said,

"… the Father hath not left me alone; for I do always those things that please him" (John 8:29).

In other words, the thoughts, words, and works of Christ made for praise, which the Father inhabited. That is what Paul and Silas consciously did; they knew how to maintain a "God friendly" atmosphere in their trying period, persecution, or difficulty. Any atmosphere which praises God (as you have seen from our definition of praise) is an atmosphere consistent with the presence and manifestation of the Lord. So, it is said,

"…at midnight Paul and Silas prayed, and sang praises unto God: and the prisoners heard them. <u>And suddenly there was a great earthquake, so that the foundations of the prison were shaken: and immediately all the doors were opened, and every one's bands were loosed</u>" (Acts 16:25/26).

God's glory, in any place and at any time, will only be manifested to the extent to which He is praised. There will always be a manifestation of God's glory because whatever is praised is magnified. *The extent to which the believer focuses on God's glory above all else, will determine the extent of the release of spiritual activity for the blessedness of the saints and the environment.*

God always wants us to focus more on Him than on anything or anyone else. He requires that because it is by beholding Him that our being is brought into participation with His glory, and that our atmosphere becomes consistent with His person. This makes for a manifestation of His good, acceptable, and perfect will. That is what happened to Paul and Silas when they were locked up in prison. What do you think would have happened had they not prayed and sang praises? Do you think their case would have been any different? Certainly not. When things change, things change. *The believer's wisdom is one which knows how to change the right thing that brings the right changes.* Changing the atmosphere is indirectly making the atmosphere consistent with any other godly changes or experiences. Praise always changes the atmosphere.

When God's children understand the beauty of praise (which is the wisdom that makes an atmosphere consistent with the glory of God), then they will learn to silence the roaring of the earth:

But the LORD is in his holy temple: let all the earth keep silence before him (Habakkuk 2:20).

When there is an atmosphere of praise, the presence of the Lord can humble any adversary and quiet any storm; the earth is commanded to keep silent before Him; Halleluiah! Whenever God is magnified, circumstances are subdued and caused to bow in worship. We see how that worked in the case of Paul and Silas, the three Hebrew boys, and even with Daniel. The fire and the lions kept silent before the Lord; because there was an atmosphere of praise; an atmosphere of divine presence. We are made for praise because we are made for divine presence.

The Psalmist understood this and said,

"The hills melted like wax at the presence of the LORD, at the presence of the Lord of the whole earth" (Psalms 97:5).

Isn't that wonderful? Even "the hills"—*every high thing which seeks to exercise dominion or poses as an authority*, melts like wax at the presence of the LORD; halleluiah! Again, the works of the glorious presence of the Lord are described in the following verses:

"When Israel went out of Egypt, the house of Jacob from a people of strange language; Judah was his sanctuary, and Israel his dominion. <u>**The sea saw it, and fled: Jordan was driven back. The mountains skipped like rams, and the little hills like lambs.**</u> **What ailed thee, O thou sea, that thou fleddest? thou Jordan, that thou wast driven back? Ye**

mountains, that ye skipped like rams; and ye little hills, like lambs? Tremble, thou earth, at the presence of the Lord, at the presence of the God of Jacob; Which turned the rock into a standing water, the flint into a fountain of waters" (Psalms 114:1-8).

The principle is simple; *what we magnify is what dominates.* The verses we just read speak of the beauty of the manifestation of the Lord's presence, which is a product of praise. It says, "**The sea saw it [the presence], and fled: Jordan was driven back. The mountains skipped like rams, and the little hills like lambs.**" What did the sea, Jordan, the mountains, and hills see? They saw the presence of the Lord. Things take their rightful place at the presence of the Lord; circumstances are humbled at the presence of the Lord. Then the Psalmist asked why the mountains skipped like rams and the hills like lambs. When he realized that it was because of the presence of the Lord, he declared, "**…Tremble, thou earth, <u>at the presence of the Lord</u>, at the presence of the God of Jacob.**"

Praise is the atmosphere of the Lord's presence; praise generates the fragrance which makes manifest the glory of God. When that is done, the Psalmist says even the rock is turned into standing water and the flint into a fountain of waters. Praise the Lord!

Therefore, the believer who places value on the praise of God has mastered the wisdom of a divine atmosphere—*the atmosphere which makes manifest the glory of God.* Praise is the atmosphere God is attracted to; it is the atmosphere of glory which attracts the most excellent experiences of God. That is the atmosphere the Psalms One man maintained; planted by the rivers of water, bearing fruits in and out of season, not knowing when heat comes, and with leaves that never go dry. It is the atmosphere of the dew of heaven, which keeps everything ever fresh and flourishing. Such an atmosphere is created by the one thing that is needful—*the walk in God's Word, which is a walk in the Spirit.*

There are five key activities in the light of the Word, which create a personal divine atmosphere for the manifestation of the glory of God. And every one of them is aimed at maintaining the atmosphere of the Lord's praise, which is the atmosphere of His presence.

5 Ways to Master Your atmosphere

1. Master Your Atmosphere by Wearing a Righteous Mind

Now thanks be unto God, which always causeth us to triumph in Christ, and <u>maketh manifest the savour of his knowledge by us in every place</u> (2 Corinthians 2:14).

A man is judged by what he thinks first, before he is judged by what he does. *From God's divine perspective, if it is in a man's thoughts, then it is as good as what is done.*

If you have been cultivating a generous mind, then you must have noticed that when you desire to do good, provision comes your way. That is the working of the law of attraction. This law is put to work by having the divine will. *The divine will (of love) attracts divine provision, because a good thought in God's sight is as good as a good deed.* For as a man thinks in his heart, so is he (Proverbs 23:7). If God looks at the heart while man looks at the act, then God reacts before man.

Do not wait to have enough to think of doing good. Think good to have enough to do good.

It is written,

"For if there be <u>first a willing mind</u>, it is accepted according to that a man hath, and not according to that he hath not" (2 Corinthians 8:12).

A mind that is first willing towards God will have its acts accepted by God. God is first interested in the state of the mind, and not the weight of the act; He approves the willing mind before an act. The act is oftentimes late to God; the mind already did it. The good thought in mind is what creates the atmosphere that God delights in. *"…If there be first, a willing mind, …"* the verse says.

The activities of your mind will always decide the activities and approval of your life. It is possible that certain things may not be resonating towards you because they are not yet in your mind; they have not inspired your will yet. And a lot may be resonating favourably towards you now because there is the aroma of a willing mind making for the favourable atmosphere around your life. *Good things are always looking for genuinely good and submissive minds towards God.*

So, Paul the apostle said, **"LET THIS MIND BE IN YOU, which was also in Christ Jesus …"** (Philippians 2:5).

This mind of Christ is a righteous mind; it is a mind that thinks of yourself and of others as God wants you to think. This is a great mind, because it thinks in alignment with God's righteousness; it has taken upon itself the position of service; it is a love-driven mind. The mind of Christ is a mind of greatness, because it takes the position of a servant, and willing to do good; it is always thinking good in humility; it is a mind which is meek and lowly.

That's why Paul the apostle said,

"Finally, brethren, whatsoever things are true, whatsoever things are honest, whatsoever things are just, whatsoever things are pure, whatsoever things are lovely, whatsoever things are of good report; if there be any virtue, and if there be any praise, <u>think on these things</u>" (Philippians 4:8).

The greatest changes you seek in life will begin in your mind—*how and what you think*. True change does not start with what men see, but with what men do not see—*the content of the mind*. The real man is not known through the things the eyes can see; no. The real man is who his mind says he is. *It is important that you learn to trigger your tangible changes by valuing intangible changes; produce your visible changes by invisible changes.*

A man's righteousness starts first in his mind. This is what Paul the apostle meant when he said,

"…For <u>with the heart man believeth unto righteousness</u>; and with the mouth confession is made unto salvation" (Romans 10:10).

When the disposition and content of the mind (the heart) is aligned in righteousness, not only are a man's steps influenced in the same, but his heart as well begins to attract the right resources, people, opportunities, and experiences.

Believing & Righteousness: Believing is aligning or shifting. When a man believes the gospel, he shifts his thinking by embracing a new way of seeing God and himself. That new state of mind or way of "seeing" is called righteousness, because it aligns with what God has done and how God sees.

The thought that dominates your mind the most becomes a garment you have permanently put on. This equally makes for a man's permanent or steady experiences. Thoughts decide a man's company; they decide his friends and enemies, his righteousness and unrighteousness. A sound mind is as a garment of many colours; it is like the streams that flow from the throne of God; it is an aroma of the heavenly which makes manifest the virtues of divinity in a man. This mind has put on Christ—*its content is inspired by who Christ is*; it attracts what Christ attracts and resists what Christ resists. That is a righteous mind; it is one aligned with God's opinion of self, things, and circumstances.

You can decide your flavour or aroma at any time by the quality of your thoughts. You can put on a heavenly aroma by thinking righteous thoughts, thereby creating a favourable atmosphere around your life.

2. Master your Atmosphere by Speaking Right Words

Words are stronger in effect over a man than his thoughts. They are very effective at making thoughts stick. Whenever you find it difficult to keep your mind on something, use your words to assist you; use words as an anchor for the thought to hold onto. Before God made the mouth to eat, He made it to speak. We have so much used the mouth to communicate with others, that we give very little attention to communicating with ourselves. A man's words have a strong effect over his mind; it influences the invisible realm and judgment passed towards him. That is why Paul the apostle said,

"...with the mouth confession is made unto salvation" (Romans 10:10).

The words of the mouth can inspire the aroma of the mind and help to maintain the thoughts of the mind. The thoughts that stay will decide the experiences that stay. What keeps coming to mind is deciding what a man keeps attracting. Your words will help keep the thoughts in mind, and consequently maintain your quality and attraction; words, just like thoughts, sow the seeds that create a man's atmosphere. Words are links to images; they will help improve the quality of the mind based on the quality of the picture the word is linking the mind to, or referencing. To maintain the garment of the mind, maintain confession of the Word. To maintain the garment of the mind, is to maintain the fragrance, which decides the atmosphere.

What you keep saying, the mind keeps seeing.

That is the reason counsel was given to Joshua the man of God to help him maintain a sound mind (a righteous mind) by speaking out God's Words. It was said, "…**this book of the law shall not depart out of thy mouth**…" (Joshua 1:8). In other words, he was to keep saying it, so his mind could keep seeing it, and as a consequence he will keep doing it.

Your words can greatly influence the sanctification of your mind. *The confession of your mouth is deciding the purging of your mind.* What you keep saying will create the garment that your mind puts on.

Your "I" confessions are your most effective confessions. Choose to use words to enforce the quality of your mind in righteousness, to keep a divine mental aroma and consequently, attract divine favour. Keep saying what God's Word has declared you to be in Christ.

Wisdom speaking in Proverbs 8:8 says,

"All the words of my mouth are in righteousness; there is nothing froward or perverse in them."

Isn't that beautiful? Words are substances in the spirit; they are either life or death. Every substance has its fragrance; a fragrance of life or death. And that in itself decides what becomes of a man's atmosphere. If there is no froward thing in a man's words, and all his words are in righteousness, then his atmosphere is one of praise! The Lord Jesus Christ said,

"It is the spirit that quickeneth; the flesh profiteth nothing: the words that I speak unto you, they are spirit, and they are life" (John 6:63).

Every word carries a message; every word is an association to something or to an experience. Words make for what becomes of a man's praise. Something you keep saying keeps releasing a fragrance which decides your atmosphere. God has given us His Word so that it should become our meditation, our confession, and consequently, our experience. Words make the atmosphere consistent with that which the Father desires for us. If we want it, we have got to keep saying it, because praise is the result of a thing being amplified by repetition, emphasis, or focus. Speaking forth God's Word is praising the Lord.

For verily I say unto you, That whosoever shall say unto this mountain, Be thou removed, and be thou cast into the sea; and shall not doubt in his heart, but shall believe that those things which he saith shall come to pass; <u>he shall have whatsoever he saith</u> (Mark11:23).

If we will have whatever we say, then what we are saying is deciding what is becoming of the atmosphere we create, and consequently what is attracted. We end up having it because words brought it forth. So, Paul the apostle says,

"Let no corrupt communication proceed out of your mouth, but that which is good to the use of edifying, that it may minister grace unto the hearers" (Ephesians 4:29).

Men are a product of their conversations. Their change decides the atmosphere and the atmosphere decides who and what is present or absent. Not only can you change your atmosphere with your words, but also the atmosphere of others. You see, Paul the apostle says do not let any "corrupt communication" (wrong words) come out of your mouth. That is because they are certainly going to have an effect on you, on your atmosphere, and on the atmosphere of others. Paul admonished that we only speak that which would edify and minister grace to those who hear us. Which means, to be in possession of the right words is to be in possession of the tools which create right atmospheres. If you can change someone's atmosphere by your words, you can change their experience. Think about that.

It is said,

"The Lord GOD hath given me the tongue of the learned, that I should know <u>how to speak a word in season to him that is weary</u>: he wakeneth morning by morning, he wakeneth mine ear to hear as the learned" (Isaiah 50:4).

You can actually change a weary man's life by your words; by right words or seasonal words. A learned tongue is one which creates a righteous atmosphere; an atmosphere which attracts the goodness of the Lord. Just like wisdom says,

"A man hath joy by the answer of his mouth: and a word

spoken in due season, how good is it!" (Proverbs 15:23).

Joy can actually come to you by the choice of words you speak. *Seasonal words are good words because they create a seasonal atmosphere.* Halleluiah! You can have such words, either by speaking what is written or what is given to you by the Spirit, even at the place of prayer. If the enemy would not change your words, he cannot change your atmosphere and consequently, he cannot influence your experiences. Because words are this delicate to a man's atmosphere and experience, the Psalmist says,

"… I will take heed to my ways, that I sin not with my tongue: I will keep my mouth with a bridle, while the wicked is before me" (Psalms 39:1).

A great part of all the wrongs that can happen in a man's life, happen first, as a result of his words. *A man who keeps his words right, keeps his life right.* Sin is of the tongue; *it is the result of corrupt words.* The Psalmist says I will keep my mouth with a bridle (and be careful with what I say), while the wicked is before me. Why? Because the wicked wants access; he gains it via the atmosphere your words create. The wicked want you to change your atmosphere by your words and make it consistent with what he is attracted to, so that he can step in lawfully. So, the Psalmist says,

"… I will take heed to my ways, that I sin not with my tongue: I will keep my mouth with a bridle, while the wicked is before me" (Psalms 39:1).

Why was he careful with his tongue before the wicked? Because wrong words were going to make the atmosphere consistent with wicked works. James the apostle also speaks of the delicate role of the tongue and the power of our words saying,

"For in many things we offend all. If any man offend not in word, the same is a perfect man, and able also to bridle the whole body" (James 3:2).

In other words, a man who masters words can move anything in the right direction, regardless of its weight. He says right talking can move your life in the right direction, because it will keep you in the right atmosphere; an atmosphere that only attracts the glory of God into your life. You can control your whole body if you can control your words. Right speaking is a major way by which we master our atmosphere. *Do not say what you see, say what you want; do not say what you feel, say what God has said or is saying. Do not say what is happening, say the change you seek.* Speak the right words, and you will create the right atmosphere. Create the right atmosphere, and you have indirectly created the right changes.

3. **Master your Atmosphere by being filled with the Spirit**

Wherefore be ye not unwise, but understanding what <u>the will of the Lord</u> is. And be not drunk with wine, wherein is excess; <u>but be filled with the Spirit</u>; Speaking to yourselves in psalms and hymns and spiritual songs, singing and making melody in your heart to the Lord; Giving thanks always for all things unto God and the Father in the name of our Lord Jesus Christ; (Ephesians 5:17-20).

The verses above begin by cautioning the believer not to be ignorant, but to understand what the will of the Lord is. That tells us there is something the Lord has provided us as wisdom and expects us to walk in. Paul the apostle goes ahead to contrast wine and the Spirit, meaning they can both make you drunk. He cautions the believer not to make wine his priority above the need to be filled with the Spirit of God. This is too vital to the believer, for the believer is given the Spirit of God as a drink; believers are to drink of the Spirit in order to be effective in their walk in God's purposes. So, we hear the Psalmist say,

"Thou preparest a table before me in the presence of mine enemies: thou anointest my head with oil; <u>my cup runneth over</u>" (Psalms 23:5).

"*...my cup runneth over...*" means there is some drinking (or filling) to be done. The same way wine intoxicates, so the Spirit of God; it becomes the main influencer of the believer's life and movements. Just as a man under the influence of alcohol no longer has a firm mastery of his steps, so also is the man full of the Spirit. The man full of the Spirit is propelled by the Spirit into action, and consequently is one with the atmosphere of God's glory. Whenever we are full of the Spirit, our atmosphere is at its best spiritual fragrance, reflecting a due season for the best of experiences.

How to be filled with the Spirit

In Ephesians 5:17-20, Paul the apostle tells us what to do to be filled with the Spirit.

1. By Speaking to yourself

"...Speaking to yourselves in psalms and hymns and spiritual songs, ..." (Ephesians 5:19). "Speaking to yourselves" does not mean speaking to others; no. It means speaking to yourself. Others cannot drink, and we get drunk, and neither can you drink, and others get drunk. Speaking to ourselves is the way we get filled with the Spirit; that is saturating our spirit with the consciousness of God's Word, promises, or praises. Paul the apostle says when we speak to ourselves, we are drinking. And that is very important.

In the natural realm, we <u>take in</u> to be filled. But in the Spirit, we <u>speak out</u> to be filled. That is worth retaining. So, he said to be filled, <u>we speak</u> to ourselves. That is how our spirits take in or drink of the Spirit. What we say decides what fills us. So, the Lord Jesus Christ said,

"Not that which goeth into the mouth defileth a man; <u>but that</u> <u>which cometh out of the mouth</u>, this defileth a man" (Matthew 15:11).

You see, whether or not we are drained or filled with the Spirit is decided by the quality of the words that come out of our mouths. Not every believer has come to understand that we are strengthened by what we say, and that not speaking God's Word will keep you weak. A man is defiled (corrupted or weakened) by what he says. Does not that go well with the Proverb 18:21;

"Death and life are in the power of the tongue: and <u>they that</u> <u>love it shall eat the fruit thereof</u>"

Why will they eat the fruit thereof? Because we are made of what we say; our words are first for us before being for anyone else.

Whether or not we are filled with death or life, is up to us. Think about this. What delicate responsibility given to man! What power within the reach of all men! If you will be filled with the Spirit and set the tone of your atmosphere, you must learn to speak to yourself as Paul the apostle said; that is how to drink of the Spirit. He tells us what to speak to ourselves; he says in psalms and hymns, and spiritual songs. Did you see that? Not all songs fill you up spiritually with life! There are "spiritual songs"—*songs born of the Spirit of God*; these are Word-rich songs; they are the kind of songs that get you drunk in the Spirit. Halleluiah!

2. By Singing and making melody in your heart

That is the next thing Paul the apostle says. He said, "…**singing and making melody in your heart to the Lord; …**" You see, speaking words to oneself is not enough; we are expected to take it further and go deeper by singing those words and even humming melodies in our hearts. Halleluiah! He says do this UNTO THE LORD. In other words, make the Lord the focus of these things; let this be about the Lord; let it be about the beauty of His love, the greatness of His power, and the excellence of His grace. The good thing is, even if you are unable to speak these things out because of the environment you may find yourself at a given time, Paul the apostle says you can "make melody in your heart". Praise

God! No one has to hear the words; spirit-filled melodies can fill you up in the Spirit. You see, all of these deal with words spoken from within you; they speak of the spiritual activities going on within you. That is how we drink spiritually, saturating our being with the consciousness of the Father's love and presence.

3. By Giving Thanks

Did you know that by a lifestyle of thanksgiving the believer can stay full of the Spirit? Murmuring and complaining drain the believer, keeping him dry. Everything that brings joy, causes the believer's life to flourish. This is because it unlocks the well of the Spirit to flow through the believer, until he or she is filled. On the other hand, you cannot murmur and be joyful at the same time, neither can you murmur and be thankful at the same time. We can only drink of one well at a time; either the well of a sorrowful heart or the well of the joy of the Lord. Joy is a major requirement for the believer's thankfulness. Thankfulness is the expression of the joy of the Spirit. But the joy of the Spirit is the result of meditating on the Lord. Thoughts basically decide our feelings or emotions. Being thankful or being ungrateful is the result of consciousness. The Psalmist says,

"My meditation of him shall be sweet: I will be glad in the

LORD" (Psalms 104:34).

Halleluiah! We can meditate on the LORD and be glad. Gladness is a product of sweet memories. And "He" (the LORD) is sweet to think about. Whether we are glad or sad, they are products of meditation. We can switch from one to another by choosing what or who to meditate on. If it is meditation on the Lord, then your heart would be sweet; you will be glad. It is when we begin to behold the graciousness of the Lord towards us, even by meditation on Him—*His Word*, that joy begins to rise in our hearts, resulting in us being thankful. Our thankfulness in this context is proven by the graciousness of our own words towards the Lord, which in return, cause us to be filled with the Spirit. That is why Paul the apostle says, "...**Giving thanks always for all things unto God and the Father in the name of our Lord Jesus Christ; ...**" (Verse 20).

So, you see, a believer full of the Spirit will create a favourable atmosphere for the manifestation of the glory of the Lord. We get filled with the Spirit by speaking to ourselves, by singing and making melody in our hearts, and by giving thanks unto the Lord. You can make this your spiritual practice and watch the glorious changes take place.

4. Master your Atmosphere by Setting your affection on things Above

Paul the apostle speaking says,

"For they that are after the flesh do mind the things of the flesh; but they that are after the Spirit the things of the Spirit. For to be carnally minded is death; but to be spiritually minded is life and peace" (Romans 8:5/6).

The above verses are worth our attention and meditation. *A man has to mind something before doing it.* The life and death mentioned in verse 6 above, are the results of either the activity of righteousness or unrighteousness. Atmospheres are not only created by thoughts, but also by actions. There are certain atmospheres which end at the thought level, and others which come forth by the activities of a man's life—*his actions.* In the verses above, Paul the apostle is not just dealing with what a man thinks, but also with the way a man lives. Righteousness in this context is living (acting) according to the Word of God; it involves conducting oneself in a manner that is consistent with what God approves. Every action according to God's Word, creates an atmosphere for the manifestation of God's glory. That is the reward of righteousness.

So, when Paul the apostle speaks of minding the things of the flesh, he is in fact referring to a way of life given to the dictates of the flesh. In other words, letting your life be ruled by your flesh, instead of being ruled by your spirit. This is proven by the way a man lives. Then he says being ruled by the flesh is being carnally minded and being ruled by the Spirit is being spiritually minded. He is basically dealing with what a man's interests are, proven by his activities. He says carnally mindedness "creates" death, while being spiritually minded "creates" life and peace. These are the actions of a man's life which decide what atmosphere is created and what consequently gets promoted; death, or life and peace.

Speaking to the saints at Colossae, Paul said,

"If ye then be risen with Christ, <u>seek those things which are above</u>, where Christ sitteth on the right hand of God. <u>Set your affection on things above</u>, not on things on the earth" (Colossians 3:1/2).

The instructions are clear; "Seek those things which are above and set your affection on things above." That is the same line of thought as being spiritually minded or carnally minded; he is dealing with our activities of interest, our way of life, our priorities, and the things we are interested in. *Every action releases a fragrance; if it is an action influenced by the Spirit, then the atmosphere becomes consistent with goodness, and if influenced by the flesh then the atmosphere is made consistent with evil.* But to the believer, he says, "...**seek those things which are above...**" In other words, let your priorities and way of life be in pursuit of the heavenly life or interests. Then he adds, "...**set your affection on things above...**" Why? So that you maintain an above atmosphere. You cannot be "above" driven and have a "beneath" atmosphere. Seeking the things above and setting your affections on things above is wisdom; that is the way of life to the wise, whereby he escapes from hell beneath. Praise the Lord!

The way of life is above to the wise, that he may depart from hell beneath (Proverbs 15:24).

So, the moment your passion or affection is set on the interest of God's Kingdom or life in Christ, and proven by your way of life, priorities, or actions, then you are mastering your spiritual atmosphere; you are intentionally creating for yourself an atmosphere consistent with the glory of God; you have escaped from "hell" (the atmosphere of evil) which is for those beneath—*those minding the affairs of the flesh.* It is said,

"For <u>he that will love life, and see good days,</u> let him refrain his tongue from evil, and his lips that they speak no guile: Let

him eschew evil, and do good; let him seek peace, and ensue it. For the eyes of the Lord are over the righteous, and his ears are open unto their prayers: but the face of the Lord is against them that do evil. And <u>who is he that will harm you, if ye be followers of that which is good</u>? But and if ye suffer for righteousness' sake, happy are ye: and be not afraid of their terror, neither be troubled;" (1 Peter 3:10-14).

Did you see that? "**And who is he that will harm you, if ye be followers of that which is good?**" And if at all righteousness produces suffering, then it is a blessing; for there is nothing to fear or to be troubled about. The Lord keeps His own in His arms. Amen. In God, there is a safe atmosphere for the righteous; the glory of God is their defence. That was what Shadrach, Meshach, and Abednego experienced. They did not sing, they did not pray; they just obeyed the Word of God; they walked in righteousness, and consequently enjoyed the safety and beauty of a divine atmosphere.

Remember, that a walk in God's Word is a walk in His presence. Every response to the Word of God leads only in the path of God's presence, and consequently in His atmosphere of glory. So, setting your affection on things above and letting your life be passionately driven by the righteousness of God is the way believers demonstrate mastery of their spiritual atmosphere. And who is he that will harm you, if you be followers (doers) of that which is good?

5. Master your Atmosphere by Walking in love

John, the apostle of Christ writes to the Church saying,

"And we have known and believed the love that God hath to us. God is love; and <u>he that dwelleth in love dwelleth in God, and God in him</u>" (1 John 4:16).

The love walk is the safest walk in the whole universe. The verse above says by walking in love, the believer dwells in God and God in him! What beats that? What other way of life is better than walking in love and dwelling in God? To dwell in God is to have God's atmosphere around you; it maintains a walk in the paths of life. What cannot penetrate God's atmosphere surely cannot reach the believer walking in love. What God therefore attracts will also be attracted to you.

To walk in love is to walk in God's seasons and enjoy God's experiences. *A walk in love sows godly seeds for a godly harvest.* Never be deceived; the power of your atmosphere is under your control.

How you live is a direct result of where you choose to walk, what seasons you submit to, and what atmospheres you create.

But he that hateth his brother <u>is in darkness</u>, and walketh in darkness, and knoweth not whither he goeth, because that darkness hath blinded his eyes (1 John 2:11).

We see that our love walk can decide where we are at a given time and what becomes of our experiences. When Satan wants an atmosphere of evil, he promotes hate amongst a people. Anything away from love moves a person into the dark and causes him to stumble. We have seen thus far that the dark places of the earth are full of the habitations of cruelty (Psalms 74:20). A love reaction is the light switch; it is a step into the light where there is no occasion for stumbling. The Lord Jesus Christ desiring that we maintain the light atmosphere said,

"A new commandment I give unto you, That ye love one another; as I have loved you, that ye also love one another" (John 13:34).

That was the divine wisdom to walk in God and keep a divine atmosphere—*an atmosphere that would ensure that things constantly worked in their favour.* Love is the winning nature and character of God. They could choose whether or not to walk in love; it was a decision they had to make and it was not some emotional decision; it was a Word-driven decision as to do what is right in God's sight. Love keeps the adversity in check; love keeps the light on; it keeps darkness under control at all times. Think about it. The love atmosphere is the glory atmosphere; it is the winning and a triumphing atmosphere. This is a major choice we always have to make in life; to hate or to love. *Everyone who loves smells like God, because he has decided to wear the godly aroma.* And if atmosphere decides attraction, the loving person can only attract glory—*the perfect will of the Father.*

He that loveth his brother <u>abideth in the light</u>, and there is none occasion of stumbling in him (1 John 2:10).

"In the light" speaks of a divine personality; it is being that which God is, and having that which God has. This makes for the ability to walk in a divine atmosphere. If a man does not abide in the light, then he abides in the dark. A man in the dark and one in the light; are both exposed to similar experiences? Certainly not. Place decides seasons, seasons decide atmosphere and atmosphere decides attractions. They cannot have the same experiences. To walk the love walk is to walk from your true self in Christ; it is to walk in truth; it is to abide in the light. From that place and by this walk in your true self in Christ, you experience God's good, acceptable, and perfect will. In the love walk, a person always triumphs, come what may.

And we know that <u>all things work together for good to them that love God,</u> to them who are the called according to his purpose" (Romans 8:28).

The love walk is a conscious walk under "the Sun" of God. The rays from "the Sun" are an enemy to sicknesses and diseases, and to every form of darkness; the life it emits is an enemy to death. It is an atmosphere which provides no habitations for cruelty; hence cruelty has no room. Praise God! Think of the peace and prosperity that can exist in a home, family, community, and nation, when believers carry such an atmosphere. The whole world is at the mercy of a love-driven people with a God-friendly atmosphere. Families and communities won't get better unless such a people arise and shine; unless believers master the glory of their atmosphere.

I beseech you therefore, brethren, by the mercies of God, that ye present your bodies a living sacrifice, holy, acceptable unto God, which is your reasonable service. And be not conformed to this world: but be ye transformed by the renewing of your mind, <u>that ye may prove what is that good, and acceptable, and perfect, will of God</u> (Romans 12:1/2).

A people who love are a people whose bodies are yielded to God as a living sacrifice, to give expression to His purpose. They are committed to responding to life and circumstances the God-way. Choose to walk in love at all times; it is the way to avoid having in you that which belongs to the prince of this world. Jesus said,

"…the prince of this world cometh, and hath nothing in me" (John14:30).

There was no room for the "prince of this world" to have a free day; the atmosphere was not one he would love to stay in; it was one saturated with love. It gave no space to bitterness, hate, anger, jealousy, lust, etc. Have a look at 1 Corinthians 13 to see the characteristics of this love—*love which when embraced, makes for the atmosphere of glory.*

Love suffereth long, and is kind; charity envieth not; love vaunteth not itself, is not puffed up, Doth not behave itself unseemly, seeketh not her own, is not easily provoked, thinketh no evil; Rejoiceth not in iniquity, but rejoiceth in the truth; Beareth all things, believeth all things, hopeth all things, endureth all things (1 Corinthians 13:4-7).

Halleluiah! Love celebrates and promotes one another in righteousness. Love is the yoke of Christ; it is not what believers should put on and put off; no. Love is the result of meekness and lowliness of heart received by learning of Christ. *A walk in love is the most authentic proof of the knowledge of Christ.* It is the pathway to greatness in the kingdom. In fact, he who loves is great. And this love is proven by serving the Lord—*by doing according to His Word.*

"…he that is greatest among you shall be your servant" (Matthew 23:11).

"Take my yoke upon you, and learn of me; for I am meek and lowly in heart: and ye shall find rest unto your souls" (Matthew 11:29).

An atmosphere of love-driven service is an atmosphere of greatness; such an atmosphere only makes manifest the perfect will of God. *To maintain a spiritual atmosphere full of glory, you must maintain on you the yoke of Christ, which is proven by a lifestyle of love-driven service.* The atmosphere of love is the atmosphere of service; and the atmosphere of service is a restful atmosphere. No other responsibility is placed on our shoulders, but that of walking in love towards God. This is proven by our service towards men.

No man hath seen God at any time. <u>If we love one another, God dwelleth in us, and his love is perfected in us</u> (1 John4:12).

If a man say, I love God, and hateth his brother, he is a liar: <u>for he that loveth not his brother whom he hath seen</u>, how can he love God whom he hath not seen? (1 John 4:20).

<u>Owe no man any thing, but to love one another</u>: for he that loveth another hath fulfilled the law (Romans 13:8).

To love is the believer's daily debt; it can never be fully paid. *Where love is, God rules*. This is the yoke of Christ which every believer ought to carry on a daily basis; it ought to be the motive in every moment and for every pursuit. It creates a safe atmosphere; it is the believer's atmosphere, the atmosphere which makes manifest the most excellent experiences God desires for His children. Love works make for the light of the world; the light in a world trapped in darkness. Men will not glorify God, until the works of love are known through the sons of God. And much more in our present world, a love walk is required.

Let your light so shine before men, that they may see your good works, and glorify your Father which is in heaven (Matthew 5:16).

The Law of Proportionality

The law of proportionality demands that it be to every man according to the level of his involvement or participation. Whether your cup runs over or not, is up to you. Good measure, pressed down, shaken together, or running over are levels of harvest, proportional to a man's seed (Luke 6:38). It is written,

"… He which soweth sparingly shall reap also sparingly; and he which soweth bountifully shall reap also bountifully" (2 Corinthians 9:6).

"… For with the same measure that ye mete withal it shall be measured to you again" (Luke 6:38).

Given that sowers who sow sparingly get a sparing harvest, and bountiful sowers get a bountiful harvest, how committed would you want to be towards these things? That is a decision you must make; sparing or bountiful harvest is up to you. To the measure you commit, you will see the glory of God; **"…with the same measure that ye met …it shall be measured to you…"** The extent of your commitment to mastering your atmosphere as a believer matters; that responsibility is given to you and I.

In Christ, our speed of change is relative; God has not set a limit for any man; we are heirs of God and join-heirs with Christ. It is written;

"But we all, with open face beholding as in a glass the glory of the Lord, are changed into the same image from glory to glory, even as by the Spirit of the Lord" (2 Corinthians 3:18).

The law of relatively decides what level of change a person gets to experience, based on the level of his investments. The glory of Christ has no limit. A man who "beholds" the glory of the Lord for ten minutes will not change as the man who beholds the glory for an hour. Remember, sparing sowing, sparing reaping; bountiful sowing, bountiful reaping. This choice is given to man; to decide how much he want. Think about this. Again, the Lord God speaking says,

"I am the LORD thy God, which brought thee out of the land of Egypt: open thy mouth wide, and I will fill it" (Psalms 81:10).

God can fill anything, depending on how widely open it is. If we open a little, we get a little. If we open wide, we get in more. The weight of glory we get to walk in, is dependent on the value we place on our spiritual atmosphere and our commitment to our spiritual walk.

CHAPTER SEVEN

RESPONDING TO AN ATMOSPHERE

The same heard Paul speak: who stedfastly beholding him, and perceiving that he had faith to be healed, (Acts 14:9).

Atmospheres tell us what to expect; they tell us what is possible if the right thing is done. As seen earlier, atmospheres reveal the seasons. Seasons tell us what is expected or what is to be done. *Success is the result of meeting the expectations of a season;* it is the result of doing the right thing at the right time. That is why wisdom says,

"...a wise man's heart discerneth both time and judgment" (Ecclesiastes 8:5).

When does the best happen? This is the question of a wise heart. If everything is made beautiful in its time (God's time), then knowing God's time (season) is necessary for sowing (responding) in accordance with the demands or requirements of the time, for the right results to come forth. *To miss out on time would be to miss out on opportunity.* But how do we know time, until we give attention to atmospheres? The atmosphere reveals the season; an atmosphere is evidence that a certain place is ready for a certain seed or action. When that seasonal seed is sown or an action is performed within that season according to the indications of the atmosphere, then desired experiences will occur. We have seen thus far, and it is worth emphasizing that atmospheres must be responded to, otherwise, they will pass by without any good or profitable changes.

The Bible gives us a scenario of a certain impotent man at Lystra, who responded to a favourable atmosphere and experienced the miracle which he had probably desired all his life:

And there sat a certain man at Lystra, impotent in his feet, being a cripple from his mother's womb, who never had walked: The same heard Paul speak: who stedfastly beholding him, and perceiving that he had faith to be healed, Said with a loud voice, Stand upright on thy feet. And he leaped and walked (Acts 14:8-10).

Isn't that wonderful? When we understand seasons and atmospheres, then we will understand that even miracles have laws. As it is required of anything that would succeed, even so it is with miracles; they follow the law of seedtime and harvest. A miracle is a harvest; it is the result of a seed sown (faith response) within the due season. Acts 14 as seen above is a typical example. First, Paul the apostle influenced the season by the activity of the Word. We know that faith comes by hearing and hearing by the Word of God (Romans 10:17). We are told that he was listening to Paul speak [the Word]. When the Word made the season ready, it was time for a response. However, men would probably not know that the season is right for sowing, unless they are able to perceive that from the atmosphere. Though this man could not perceive that the atmosphere was right for his response, Paul the apostle knew it was his season—*his due time.*

This impotent man, even though he had the faith to be healed, did not know how to respond to his due atmosphere for a miracle. He did not know how to work out his faith. Imagine that Paul the apostle had been unable to perceive his faith; the miracle will not have occurred, even though it was the right season. Places remain barren when they do not receive a seed in season. Sowing in season is faith well used; sowing in season is righteousness.

It is important to understand that a faithless response in due season can be just as futile as a bad seed in good soil. The atmosphere can be right, but the response that would be fruitful ought to be one inspired by the Word of God. That is faith indeed. In this case, the presence of faith was an indication of a right season, because it was created in the atmosphere of the Word. But just as the iron must be hit when it is hot, one must know that the iron is hot, so that the seed-action (righteousness) can be carried out, in order for the harvest of a new shape to occur. Paul the apostle saw that this man "had faith to be healed." In other words, it was the right season, and this man had the required seed. So, he helped him respond to his season;

"The same heard Paul speak: who stedfastly beholding him, and perceiving that he had faith to be healed, <u>Said with a loud voice, Stand upright on thy feet. And he leaped and walked</u>."

Praise the Lord! "He leaped and walked" is the harvest; that was the new experience he got. But then, what was the seed? If a miracle is a harvest, then what is the seed? Success is no mystery; it is simple. Success is the result of planting the right seed, in the right season. It is one thing to have an expectation, it is another to respond when the season is right. The ability to identify the atmosphere, so that you can tell your season, is crucial to experiencing success in life. It is very important therefore to know the state of an atmosphere. *We are either waiting for the atmosphere to know the season, or influencing the season to sow the right seeds.* The Lord Jesus Christ rebuking a certain people for being ignorant about atmospheres and consequently not knowing how to maximize their seasons, said:

"For the days shall come upon thee, that thine enemies shall cast a trench about thee, and compass thee round, and keep thee in on every side, And shall lay thee even with the ground, and thy children within thee; and they shall not leave in thee one stone upon another; because thou knewest not the time of thy visitation" (Luke 19:43/44).

It is acceptable to say at this point, that a missed season is a missed experience. The odd experiences were to happen to the people mentioned above because they did not know THE TIME of their visitation. Think about that: *In life, we are either creating an atmosphere for others to sow into us, or identifying an atmosphere to sow into.* Remember that atmospheres occur in places; you are a place, and so is your business. Knowing when and how to respond to an atmosphere is fundamentally what makes for a man's success.

Requirements for a Successful Response

According to Jeremiah 29:11, God's thoughts for us are good; He desires to bring us to an "expected end" (a harvest of good experiences). But that will not happen without our participation and walk in His wisdom, which governs the affairs of the earth and the Spirit. In fact, at one time the Lord spoke of the consequences of our ignorance (or lack of understanding) saying,

"They know not, <u>neither will they understand; they walk on in darkness:</u> all the foundations of the earth are out of course" (Psalms 82:5).

God does not want us to lack understanding, because that will result in us walking in darkness. It is not enough to confess God's promises; that is why this book was written; to provide understanding of how things work, so that we can take advantage of that understanding and walk in God's perfect will—*in His light*. To understand how God leads and how to follow, kindly read my book "WHEN GOD LEADS." You will see that one of the major and most effective ways God leads us is by giving us understanding. A man with understanding has God's permanent light in a given domain.

So, here are three key things which are required in order to attain good success:

1. Identify your good seed(s)

Before you can take advantage of an atmosphere, you must identify your seed. Your seed is your response towards an atmosphere; it is sown in the field. Your future lies in your seed. *A man without a seed cannot create a future.* If there is a season termed "seedtime", then it is a season which expects seeds. It is the seed in season that creates the future. *Something a man has is necessary for creating what he wants.* That is really what a seed is.

It is worth noting that anything we can think, say, do, or give, is a seed; our energy, knowledge, time, and skill are seeds. Now think about this. What is it that you think? What is it that you say? What is that you do? What is it that you give? You are actually sowing. So, at any given time, every human is sowing and harvesting, even by the thoughts of the mind. That is what this world is; it is a seedtime-harvest world existing in a continuous cycle. There is never a time when someone is not sowing or harvesting. Men are full of seeds; there is no man without a seed; no man. That implies that, the least of men living, has something to sow. *He who can always sow can always change the outcome of things.* In fact, men are seeds; a man can even sow himself. The Lord Jesus Christ taught us that when He sowed Himself through His death, to bring forth the harvest of a new creation—*the sons of God.*

Paul the apostle says,

"…we speak the wisdom of God in a mystery, even the hidden wisdom, which God ordained before the world unto our glory: Which none of the princes of this world knew: for had they known it, they would not have crucified the Lord of glory" (1 Corinthians 2:7/8).

Why would they not have crucified Him had they known? Because they would have known that crucifying Him was permitting Him to seed Himself, and consequently be multiplied by His resurrection (the harvest). So, in actual fact, we do not end the life of a seed by sowing it; rather, we glorify it—*we multiply it*. That is why it is said,

"There is that scattereth, and yet increaseth; and there is that withholdeth more than is meet, but it tendeth to poverty" (Proverbs 11:24).

So, in your seed, you can see your future. The man who identifies seed has already identified the change or increase he wants to produce. God's wisdom of change begins with a seed. Where men begin to minimize or abuse seeds, they abuse changes. Wisdom begins by identifying seeds. The beautiful advantage of this to believers is that, God's Word is not just a seed, it is also a guide on how to live a life of sowing. In other words, any teaching, instruction, or counsel from God's Word, is a seed to man; it shows a man how to sow in a profitable manner.

Doing the Word of God is sowing your life in the most profitable and infallible manner. If you have God's Word (or code of conduct in life), you have the most excellent seeds for life. Do not seek for anything better than that. Doing God's Word, be it in your personal life, relationships, business, or career, is sowing the best seeds for life. Jesus said,

"If ye know these things, happy are ye if ye do them" (John 13:17).

What that means is, "happiness" is the harvest for word-doers. God's children are cautioned in a very simple yet accurate way; they are required to live by the Word, and in so doing, it will be well with them.

"Hear therefore, O Israel, and observe to do it; that it may be well with thee, and that ye may increase mightily, as the LORD God of thy fathers hath promised thee, in the land that floweth with milk and honey" (Deuteronomy 6:3).

"And thou shalt do that which is right and good in the sight of the LORD: that it may be well with thee, ..." (Deuteronomy

6:18).

"Say ye to the righteous, that it shall be well with him: for they shall eat the fruit of their doings" (Isaiah 3:10).

Anyone living by the teachings of Christ, is sowing good seeds, and it shall be well with them. Anyone instructing you is influencing your seeds and inspiring your harvest.

2. The field (Place or Soil)

Seeds stay as they are until they meet the soil. Everything remains alone unless it is planted. The present state of affairs will not change unless death is brought about by sowing. The Lord Jesus Christ taught us this saying,

"Verily, verily, I say unto you, Except a corn of wheat fall into the ground and die, <u>it abideth alone</u>: but if it die, it bringeth forth much fruit" (John 12:24).

The corn of wheat (seed) abides alone unless it falls into the ground and dies. The Lord said, it is only when that happens that it brings forth "much fruit." So, a seed is not multiplied until it is sown; experiences do not change until there is action. The ground is what will decide what becomes to the seed. The parable of the sower in Mark Chapter 4 tells us that. *As good as the quality of the seed might be, the wrong soil will disappoint the sower.* Paul the apostle also teaches us that where we sow decides what we receive (our experiences or harvest); in other words, give attention to your soil. He says,

"For he that soweth to his flesh shall of the flesh reap corruption; but he that soweth to the Spirit shall of the Spirit reap life everlasting" (Galatians 6:8).

In other words, there is the soil of the flesh and the soil of the Spirit. We can all sow into any at any given time. To learn more on the subject sowing to the Spirit, which is the believer's wisdom for distinction, kindly get my book "Sowing to the Spirit." In the book, I shared extensively on the subject of seeds and soils, as it pertains to the believer's wisdom for sufficient living.

So, fields matter. And as mentioned earlier, if people are places, then what you say, what you do, what you give and to whom, matters a great deal. It matters where you go to church and where you serve. It matters who you relate with and who you invest your life in. The same thing done towards different people cannot have the same results, just like the same business might not be successful everywhere. God's wisdom of seeds must equally give attention to "the place" for it to be productive or successful. So, we hear the

Lord say,

"Take heed to thyself that <u>thou offer not thy burnt offerings in every place that thou seest</u>: But in the place which the LORD shall choose in one of thy tribes, there thou shalt offer thy burnt offerings, and there thou shalt do all that I command thee" (Deuteronomy 12:13/14).

It is not enough to know what to do; where you do it matters. Was God concerned about the place of their seeds? Certainly, because places are not the same; they were not supposed to think just any place was good enough for their offerings. As a believer in Christ Jesus, you have to understand this, because your offerings and services will not yield the same results everywhere. Just because you have something good does not mean it can be given anywhere you want. This is the reason why some people keep giving and keep serving, but never seem to get the expected results. Their "field" or place may be wrong.

For example, certain people say they can give their tithes anywhere they want. They say it does not matter where you give it, as long as you are giving to God. They are ignorant of the disciplines of sowing to the Spirit. Did you notice from the verse we just read, that God frowns at such attitudes? That is because their offerings were not going to be productive for them, had they chosen to do it wherever they wanted. In the verse above, He says, "...**Take heed to thyself that thou offer not thy burnt offerings in every place that thou seest.**" In other words, if they were to be successful in what they were doing, then simply knowing what to do would not suffice. Where they did it would be just as important. He said, "Do it in the place that I choose." That is remarkable.

Understanding the place of your service or your activities is crucial to living a successful life, even as a believer in Christ Jesus. God is in the soil; He is ready to multiply or amplify what we do. The Bible tells us of four lepers, who stood at the gate of an impoverished city. They said to themselves; if we stay at this gate, we die. And if we move towards our adversary, they may show us mercy or kill us. In any case, the direction where mercy is an option is preferable. So, they decided to move; they acted on their faith. The Bible tells us that as they were moving towards their adversary, their adversary (the Syrians) rose up and fled. What happened? Why did they flee? We are told why:

"**For the Lord had made the host of the Syrians <u>to hear a noise of chariots, and a noise of horses, even the noise of a great host</u>: and they said one to another, Lo, the king of Israel hath hired against us the kings of the Hittites, and the kings of the Egyptians, to come upon us**" (2 Kings 7:6).

Praise the Lord! So, what the Lord amplified were the steps of these lepers; they sowed in the right direction (or place), and God gave the harvest; He multiplied their seed. That is why it is said,

"Now he that ministereth seed to the sower both minister bread for your food, <u>and multiply your seed sown</u>, and increase the fruits of your righteousness; …" (2 Corinthians 9:10).

Only sown seeds are multiplied; not withheld seeds. We know that the ground does the multiplying; it is from the ground that the power of resurrection works. Even so, God is waiting for us in the soil. For He cannot be mocked; whatever a man sows, that shall he reap (Galatians 6:5). So, God wants to give us more, but He waits for us in the soil; for even God Himself is a place; that is why we are able to sow to the Spirit.

That which a man does not desire to multiply should not be sown, and that which a man desires to multiply, should not be withheld.

Whenever you are sure of the 'seed' question, make sure you also answer the 'place' question. Yes, you have something to say, but who are you saying it to? Yes, you know what to do, but where are you doing it? If you open up your heart to this, the Holy Spirit would be your guide. Even as you give yourself to studying your productive places or fields in life; know your most fruitful place of harvest, and maximize your investments there. This is why it is important to be guided by the Spirit and to walk in the light of God's Word. Our atmosphere reveals our place when we walk in the light of God's Word.

3. The Season (or Time)

The right seed and place can be frustrated by the season. Success will not come forth unless the three are at work. Remember, wisdom says,

"…a threefold cord is not quickly broken" (Ecclesiastes 4:12).

Things can only truly work out when they are one—*in agreement*. The same applies to the wisdom of these three; seed, field, and season. When these three agree, success or quality change is inevitable. And this is where we see the vital role the atmosphere plays in revealing seasons. We covered in earlier sections the beauty of seasons. Seasons, as earlier mentioned, basically tell us what the soil is ready for. The word "ready" is vital here. In other words, until it is the right season, the soil, field, or place, is not ready for your seed. Seasons indicate that the field is ready for seeds. In other words, the right season means, all that is necessary for the field to maximize and consequently multiply the seed, is in place. That is why wisdom says,

"...a word spoken in due season, how good is it!" (Proverbs 15:23).

Good counsel to the right person out of season can be very disappointing. Remember, the three must go together. The word (the seed) may not be bad, but it is only good when spoken (planted) in season. You may have the money, the skill, the knowledge, etc.; but where and when you apply them will decide gain or loses. So, wisdom says, a word spoken in due season is good —*it is profitable.* Yes, I have my seed; yes, I know the field (or place). But, is it the right season or time? That is the last question that results in true success.

Given that the atmosphere reveals the season, if you have your seed and you know your place, all you need to do is observe the atmosphere and respond accordingly. The need to respond cannot be overemphasized. The response is the sowing part; it is the point at which the seed leaves you to the field or soil. And until it leaves, it cannot be multiplied; it cannot produce change. This is what faith is; it is doing the right thing. If we can rightly interpret the atmosphere, then we have interpreted the season. The Lord Jesus Christ said,

"Now learn a parable of the fig tree; When his branch is yet tender, and putteth forth leaves, <u>ye know that summer is nigh</u>: ..." (Matthew 24:32).

In other words, how can we tell summer is near? By observing the changes in the atmosphere; by observing the tender branch of the fig tree putting forth leaves. The Lord is by such wisdom telling us that there are always signs which reveal what season it is. It is therefore, not a hard thing to do. *No season comes unannounced; none. Seasons cannot hide, just as fruits do not hide and do not lie.* That, in effect, is what an atmosphere is; it is fruit of a season. It is perceivable; it can be identified. Every season has its characteristics; we can always learn to identify them. If you are a business person for example, there is a right season to invest. Otherwise, it can result in waste or loses. The children of Issachar whom we have seen a couple of times throughout this book were said to be,

"...men that had <u>understanding of the times</u>, to know what Israel ought to do; the heads of them were two hundred; and all their brethren were at their commandment" (1 Chronicles 12:32).

Understanding deals with interpretation. It involves relating that which is perceivable (seen, smelled, tasted, heard, or felt) to that which is unknown, so that actions can be just. To the spiritual man (or the believer), there exist such spiritual indicators too, by which he can tell that the season is right for a certain action. In studying your Bible for example, or listening to the Word of God being preached or taught in Church, there comes a time in the course of your hearing when your atmosphere changes. It changes because the season has been made right (by the ministration of the Spirit). The Spirit of the Lord will bear witness to you in diverse ways, that you are due for a certain action or experience.

Responding at that time will result in an expected change; whether in your body or in your affairs. An "Amen" at that time can be the response of faith by which you receive something made available in Christ for you. A certain word spoken at that time would be a word in season, which goes forth to create the desired changes. But you see, just like the man who was lame from birth during Paul's ministration responded, you too must respond. However, if you are not helped or taught on how best to respond to your atmosphere, miracles and changes can walk past you. Failing to respond could mean missing out on your season, even though the atmosphere was ready for change.

Moving with the Cloud

Every miracle, walk in the supernatural, or good success recorded in the Bible, were the results of people who (consciously or unconsciously) responded to their divine atmosphere. We are either creating it or responding to it. God the Father will always show us how to walk in His seasons and how to identify the seasons by our atmosphere. In fact, most times the Lord leads us using that atmosphere. This can happen by the prompting of your spirit, wherein you just know within you a certain action is due for the time. The Bible says the Spirit of the Lord bears witness with our spirits that we are sons of God (Romans 8:16). The Lord can speak to you in diverse ways regarding your time for a change. In fact, we are told of Abraham, who is an example of a man who moved as God spoke:

So Abram departed, as the LORD had spoken unto him; (Genesis 12:4).

That was not a move out of season; it was one in season. To some other person, it may be an instruction to preach, pray, or heal someone. To another, it may be an instruction to begin a business, pursue a certain career, study a certain course, get married (move out of your father's house), or just turn left or right. The beauty of prompt obedience is that we sow in season. When the season changes, the seed or action would be useless or unprofitable. That is why it is said, "Obedience is better than sacrifice."

And Samuel said, Hath the LORD as great delight in burnt offerings and sacrifices, as in <u>obeying the voice of the LORD</u>? Behold, <u>to obey is better than sacrifice</u>, and to hearken than the fat of rams (1 Samuel 15:22).

"Sacrifice" in this context is when you choose to despise a seasonal instruction, to later on (at your own time, in your own way, and at your own convenience) invest diligently in it. It does not just suffice that you did something; no. When and how you did it, is really what matters. If the iron would be sharp and ensure effort is not wasted, it has to be hit when it is hot; not when it goes cold. When sacrifice replaces obedience (responding to instructions in season), then the labour becomes difficult. Consequently, beauty will not show up as it was supposed to. It is vital to be convinced that everything can only be beautiful in its time. The ability to tell an atmosphere and move with it is golden. The Bible tells us how the Israelites made the journey through the wilderness saying,

"And the LORD went before them by day in a pillar of a cloud, to lead them the way; and by night in a pillar of fire, to give them light; to go by day and night: He took not away the

pillar of the cloud by day, nor the pillar of fire by night, from before the people" (Exodus 13:21/22).

We see here that the Israelites were led by the pillar of cloud by day and the pillar of fire by night. Therefore, if they were to enjoy light and have a smooth journey, it would have been burdensome for them to travel without considering the clouds. For the pillar of cloud and fire, were what signalled to them when it was necessary to move, and in what direction. The Lord Himself was the light of His people. This is how God wants it to be for the believer. Isaiah 60 speaks of this saying,

"The sun shall be no more thy light by day; neither for brightness shall the moon give light unto thee: but the LORD shall be unto thee an everlasting light, and thy God thy glory" (Isaiah 60:19).

Isn't that wonderful? The Lord is the light for the believer's movement. That is because the Lord will always be in season. Therefore, the believer must be in sync with Him in order to walk in God's seasons. That is why it is said,

"The spirit of man is the candle of the LORD, searching all the inward parts of the belly" (Proverbs 20:27).

In other words, God uses man's spirit to see through man's activities and to instruct what is right to be done at a given time. That is moving with the cloud. If you are sensitive to tell the atmospheres of your spirit, you can always move according to "the cloud" of the Spirit. The Lord Jesus Christ knew when it was time to offer up Himself; He could tell by changing atmospheres that the time was near. The Bible tells us that.

Then cometh Jesus with them unto a place called Gethsemane, and saith unto the disciples, Sit ye here, while I go and pray yonder. And he took with him Peter and the two sons of Zebedee, and began to be sorrowful and very heavy. <u>Then saith he unto them, My soul is exceeding sorrowful, even unto death</u>: tarry ye here, and watch with me (Matthew 26:36-38).

His sorrow was an indication that the atmosphere was changing, and the right time for Him to sow Himself was approaching. That is remarkable and worth taking note of. As God's children, we can tell by the moving cloud that our seasons are changing, and move along. If one was to find unique examples for every individual, the list would be inexhaustible. And that is why we are given the Holy Spirit; to guide us in diverse ways, unique to us. It is worth noting that the Spirit's love for us causes Him to keep pressing and alerting us until we successfully respond. So, have no worries about that; as long as you have understood this lesson and henceforth willing to be sensitive and to move as He guides, then all will be well. It is important to always tell "the time of your visitation."

It is said,

"I will go before thee, and make the crooked places straight: I will break in pieces the gates of brass, and cut in sunder the bars of iron:" (Isaiah 45:2).

That is always God's wisdom; to "go before thee and make the crooked places straight." Whenever we see our atmosphere change, we can tell that the Lord has gone before us and has made the crooked paths straight. Now, we can follow accordingly. That is what makes for the believer's exemption— *the unique results of the sons of God.*

Aligning with your Seasons

Predestination simply means God has our lives all worked out for good. All that we need for life has been fully supplied to us by the Lord. This is worth believing. God is not working out anything new for anyone of us. Before we were ever created and born into this world, all of our days were fully established in glory before Him. That is why the Psalmist says,

"Thine eyes did see my substance, yet being unperfect; and <u>in thy book all my members were written</u>, which in continuance were fashioned, <u>when as yet there was none of them.</u> How precious also are thy thoughts unto me, O God! how great is the sum of them!" (Psalms 139:16/17).

These are beautiful thoughts of hope which ought to bring joy to our hearts every time we read or think about them. The Psalmist by those words, was saying that even the parts of his body were written in God's book. If such can be of interest to God, what more of the very life and experiences of a man's life? We are not without a well-structured beautiful plan in God's book. *In fact, the believer's life is an unfolding of experiences in God's script.* That is why it is important to believe. Believing is aligning with God, ensuring that all He has already written is fulfilled. Even the Lord Jesus Christ mentioned that He came to live out all that is written of Him, saying,

"Then said I, Lo, I come: in the volume of the book it is written of me, ..." (Psalms 40:7).

The safest place any man can ever be, is in the will of God. For only in

His will does His best happen; the supply of His grace can be fully received and maximized in His will. This is why it is important to get to know the Lord and His plans, and not to be lost in making up yours. Creatures do not make up their purposes; they discover what was in the Creator's mind before they were made. What book did the Lord Jesus Christ live out? God's book of purpose. We all in this world, have our names in the book; and we walk in the light of it as it is revealed to us and as we get to believe and respond accordingly. *We are believers because we respond to the Father's ways, thoughts, or plans for us.* So, it is said,

"For I know the thoughts that I think toward you, saith the LORD, thoughts of peace, and not of evil, to give you an expected end" (Jeremiah 29:11).

And again,

"Behold, what manner of love the Father hath bestowed upon us, that we should be called the sons of God: the world knoweth us not, because it knew him not" (1 John 3:1).

You will find so much rest when you settle on the fact that God the Father has loved you with an everlasting love, and that you cannot care more about your life than He already does. When we come to this place of rest (by believing), then we cease to be under any form of pressure to attain anything or make anything work; we cease to "make haste." A man has to be pressured to make haste. On the contrary, believing brings us into His rest, where we now know that all things are worked out perfectly by the Father for our good, and that His mercies and grace ensure that we get the best of it as we place our trust in Him.

Therefore thus saith the Lord GOD, Behold, I lay in Zion for a foundation a stone, a tried stone, a precious corner stone, a sure foundation: he that believeth shall not make haste (Isaiah 28:16).

When we settle on such divine truths, we experience the beauty of Psalms 85:13:

"Righteousness shall go before him; and shall set us in the way of his steps."

That is what it means to walk in preordained paths according to Ephesians 2:10. We are made to walk according to the content of our respective books in Christ. This will happen as we rest in Him, letting His Spirit "set us in the way of His steps." Halleluiah! This is intentional living; it is the glorious reflection of the excellence of God. Haste is what takes a person out of season with God. Haste takes a man ahead of God, into places God has not been through. Consequently, he is left to deal with the crooked paths and to pave his own way. How burdensome and wearying that can be. That is the root and seat of all confusion and struggles in life. Such people have not found God's love; the love wherein He grants His children sleep, and keeps them from eating the bread of sorrows (Psalms 127:1/2). It is restful indeed to walk with God and according to His leading.

The Beauty of Faithfulness

It is said,

"A faithful man shall abound with blessings: but he that maketh haste to be rich shall not be innocent" (Proverbs 28:20).

Why is there no innocence in haste? Because the one making haste skips steps, and when a man skips steps, he skips seasons. And the man who skips seasons, falls out of the path of success or fulfilment because the necessary factors which ought to be in place for his seeds or his activity are not yet in place. Therefore, he struggles and is far from being innocent. He reaps the opposite of beauty; for things are only beautiful in their time. That is the reason he cannot claim to be innocent, as though something ugly happened to him without him being at fault. Haste (or impatience) is costly. So, wisdom says, "**A faithful man shall abound with blessings…**"

What is faithfulness?

Faithfulness is sticking to God's Word until the atmosphere becomes consistent with the next seed or action. It is being diligent in God's Word until the next phase rightly opens up. Faithfulness is being planted, fixed, and stable in your activity of truth—*the Word of God.*

It is said,

"The righteous shall flourish like the palm tree: he shall grow like a cedar in Lebanon. Those that be planted in the house of the LORD shall flourish in the courts of our God. They shall still bring forth fruit in old age; they shall be fat and flourishing; To shew that the LORD is upright: he is my rock, and there is no unrighteousness in him" (Psalms 92:12-15).

Halleluiah! See what faithfulness (being planted) can do! Isn't that wonderful? Find a faithful man, and you have found a flourishing man whose life is comparable to that of the palm tree; his faithfulness towards God has positioned him where his seasons have become God's. That is how we align ourselves with God's purposes for our lives. God does not change His place; we change ours, through unfaithfulness. Faithfulness simply gets us aligned with the unchanging God. His love for us neither increases nor decreases. Our love, on the other hand, is able to increase and decrease, which is proven by our unfaithfulness. God is not less loving in our failure than He is in our success. If we fall off, God did not leave us; we left Him. And given that He does not change, He will always be right where we left Him. By returning and being faithful, we can enjoy His goodness again. And for our shame, He always restores double to us, in order to cause us catch-up (Isaiah 61:7). That is how loving God is and how powerful faithfulness is. Faithfulness connects and maintains position in righteousness.

Faithfulness does not just wait for a season, but it also prepares a person for the season. That is why it causes a person to abound with blessings, because the faithful person is always on time and consequently having all things beautiful. It is a man's faithfulness that leads to the manifestation of his seasons. Remember that in Chapter One, we saw the practical example of Cloud Manipulation, by which a man seeds the cloud to bring forth rain. The lesson behind that is that activity can decide what becomes of a man's seasons. It is possible to manipulate your season and get yourself into another phase of life. But as wisdom stated, hasty people will not be innocent, due to the evil which will follow their "manipulation." Manipulation in this context would mean not following due protocol in a bid to arrive the good or expected end. The end will surely not be beautiful, even though you might eventually get there.

A man can manipulate his clouds through deception, lies, theft, cheating, etc., and somehow seem to get the desired season change; but it will be a phantom season, setting him up for his own doom. So, wisdom says,

"Divers weights are an abomination unto the LORD; and a false balance is not good" (Proverbs 20:23).

The above verse speaks of manipulators; people who change the standard in order to deceive and arrive quickly. The Bible calls that divers weights and false balances. *Whatever despises righteousness (or God's Word), yet brings us closer to our own desires has brought us closer to death.* Such has taken us out of God's seasons. Only mercy saves at that point. Watch a struggling or frustrated person; he is very likely not in alignment with God's seasons for his life; he is out of place. And as seen earlier,

"... Cursed be the man that trusteth in man, and maketh flesh

his arm, and whose heart departeth from the LORD. For he shall be like the heath in the desert, and shall not see when good cometh; but shall inhabit the parched places in the wilderness, in a salt land and not inhabited" (Jeremiah 17:5/6).

That is not the kind of testimony we want for ourselves as believers in Christ. Everything is beautiful when God brings us there Himself. If the place is wrong, it cannot have the best of God's atmosphere. Faithfulness is the only authentic way to rightly influence your seasons and walk in God's best. The faithful person goes with God, but the unfaithful one goes without God. If we refuse to skip steps through haste or impatience, we will always have God's best worked out in our favour. It is said,

"And we know that all things work together for good to them that love God, to them who are the called according to his purpose" (Romans 8:28).

Yes, we are called by His purpose; that is what believing has brought us into. Now our love for the Lord—*faithfulness*—is what causes all things to work out for our good; that is what makes for the unfolding of the purposes for which God has called us. Faithfulness is waiting on the Lord by being diligent with whatever

His Word says or by doing whatever has been entrusted you to do. That is trusting the Lord. And we saw earlier that trust decides a man's place. Activity in place will make for a man's seasons and experiences. It is written,

"Wait on the LORD, and keep his way, and he shall exalt thee to inherit the land: when the wicked are cut off, thou shalt see it" (Psalms 37:34).

It is neither faithfulness nor waiting on the Lord, unless a man is diligent in doing God's word or walking in righteousness. Patience in wrong-doing can only lead to more wrong. Faithfulness or waiting upon the Lord does two major things:

1- **It makes external factors consistent with God's perfect will.**

From a man's activity or diligence, his seasons are influenced. Slothfulness, idleness, or laziness never gets a person to align with God's seasons. We sow our seasons by faithfulness. No faithful person is wasting. If at any time the enemy tries to tempt you out of faithfulness, kindly remind yourself of this and remind him as well; no one who is being faithful is wasting.

2- It causes you to mature alongside the changing season.

Frustration is when a season meets an unprepared man. When God the Father is leading, He causes our maturity to match with our seasons. Therefore, it is not just about expecting external factors to align, but also trusting internal factors to align. Sometimes, we are unable to tell these changes, so we must trust God to be faithful and to open things up at the right time; we must stay the course, and not faint.

A restful life only responds to God's seasons which are always favourable. By waiting upon the Lord, we are aligning with His seasons. We will be good to go when the atmosphere changes, showing us that the season is ripe. Remember, there is no waste in faithfulness. Paul the apostle says,

"And let us not be weary in well doing: for in due season we shall reap, if we faint not" (Galatians 6:9).

That time will always come; and it always comes for the man who stays faithful and refuses to be weary. When the enemy wants to disconnect a man from aligning with God's seasons, he discourages the man. When the man is discouraged, he becomes reluctant, slothful, or idle. When activity stops, alignment with seasons has been hindered. Cloud manipulation gains its wisdom from the actual cloud seeding wisdom. The difference is that it is using alternative means from God's standard to get the cloud to respond favourably. Even so today, the devil has not stopped bringing alternatives to God's children, just like he did to Eve and even to the Lord Jesus Christ. He seeks to deviate from the one thing that works—*faithfulness towards God*. Only then can he move us out of God's will and take advantage of our ignorance or disobedience. Faithfulness does not lose; it always wins. Faithfulness will always keep a person in God's time and increase the person God's way.

If you will not stop seeding your cloud, you will not be out of season with God. There is no better alternative to waiting upon the Lord or aligning with God's own superior kingdom seasons for your life, than faithfulness. God cannot lie and He cannot be late. If you refuse to get weary in doing good— *living according to God's Word*, you will surely reap the experiences of God's perfect will, as they unfold to you according to God's good purpose for your life in His book. Then, your life will have the testimony of the path of the just, which is as a shining light that shines "**...more and more unto the perfect day**" (Proverbs 4:18). This just man is a faithful man whose faithfulness puts him in constant alignment with God's perfect will, causing him to respond correctly to his divine atmosphere and thus, receive the harvest of his seeds.

CONCLUSION

Decisions decide phases.

If ye know these things, happy are ye if ye do them (John 13:17).

Everything is said to be in a state of rest or uniform motion, except an external force is applied to it. That is called the law of motion, or the law of change. Even so your life. Good books do not necessarily make good people; good decisions do. Give your life a facelift by making a major decision today. Take the decision henceforth, you will not run your life based on your own understanding, but based on God's wisdom of place, seasons, atmosphere, and activities which this book has helped you to understand. We are always just a decision away from our glorious changes.

The verse above says your happiness is not in your hearing only, but in your doing. There is nothing small or little about God's Word. The Lord Jesus Christ describes the effect of God's Word as a mustard seed, which when planted becomes the greatest of trees. A little action on any word received from God will make great things happen. One little change or adjustment influenced by an instruction or an understanding can cause a ripple effect of good changes in your life.

There is a lot of knowledge going out in our world today, but hearers and doers [of God's Word] will be those producing significant results and walking in God's perfect will. James says,

"But be ye doers of the word, and not hearers only, deceiving your own selves" (James 1:22).

The Lord Jesus Christ Himself lived a life influenced by the leading of God the Father. He said,

"I can of mine own self do nothing: as I hear, I judge: and my judgment is just; because I seek not mine own will, but the will of the Father which hath sent me" (John 5:30).

Those are the words of a man whose life was yielded to the will of God the Father. As believers in Christ Jesus, He has given us "the way" to live as God's children — the way of being led by God, and doing according to His Word.

Via this book, God the Father has emphasized the importance of being in the right place and maximizing the beauty of seasons. A new life can begin right now by you making a firm commitment saying, *"Yes Lord, let's go. Henceforth I am going to live by this understanding."*

It is said by God's Word,

The man that wandereth out of the way of understanding shall remain <u>in the congregation of the dead</u> (Proverbs 21:16).

So, there is such a thing as the congregation of the dead. It is a place that only those who wander out of the way of understanding are permitted to dwell. But then the Psalmist says,

"Thou wilt shew me the path of life: in thy presence is fulness of joy; at thy right hand there are pleasures for evermore" (Psalms 16:11).

Having received such understanding – *the path of life*, why choose to remain in the congregation of the dead when there is the congregation of the living – *the righteous?*

Therefore the ungodly shall not stand in the judgment, nor sinners <u>in the congregation of the righteous</u> (Psalms 1:5).

The call to godliness is made to you today; no room for excuses; no time to look back. The Lord Jesus Christ said to one, follow me. And he said,

"… I will follow thee; but let me first go bid them farewell, which are at home at my house" (Luke 9:61).

And the Lord said to him,

"No man, having put his hand to the plough, and looking back, is fit for the kingdom of God" (Luke 9:62).

God's opinion should not be compared with anything else. Do not seek to finish on the wrong path before responding to God's call. If He says follow me, respond promptly. It is said hit the iron while it is hot. If the Lord has spoken to you via this book, respond to His call now. He is the first; there is no other worth considering. The man said, *"I'll follow you, but first…"* There is no "but" with God. He is calling you forward; not backward. from the time God calls, no one going back is doing the right thing.

Today can be a whole new beginning for you. Make a new decision. And that is a decision to dwell in the congregation of the righteous, and nothing else but the land of the living. A new and glorious phase lies in your decision today.

If you henceforth desire a godly life and a walk in the congregation of the righteous, you can make this decision prayer of commitment, and let a new and blessed way of life begin for you today and right now:

Dear Heavenly Father,

Today I acknowledge that he that follows you shall not walk in darkness but shall dwell in the congregation of the righteous, and enjoy the seasons and atmospheres of the kingdom. Today, I receive Christ Jesus as my Lord and my Saviour, and commit myself to be led and guided by your Spirit. I acknowledge that the life of Christ is my life; I am a son of God; a tree planted by the rivers of water which brings forth fruits in season. I am flourishing and excelling in your perfect love for me, In Jesus Name. Amen.

TO CONTACT THE AUTHOR:

Daniel Nyah Allo

Douala — Cameroon

The LightWalk Office

+237 243 858 491 (Call)

+237 654 512 218 (WhatsApp).

Email: info@danielnyah.org

www.danielnyah.org

OTHER BOOKS BY

Daniel Nyah Allo

- A BETTER LIFE IN 31 DAYS

- MAKING RICH THE POOR

- WHEN GOD LEADS

- SOWING TO THE SPIRIT

The LightWalk
Daily Devotional

Daily experience peace and good success.

The LightWalk is a daily devotional which encourages your daily experience of God's peace and a walk in good success; in your health, relationships, and daily pursuits.

 +237 654 512 218

 Lddsubscribe@gmail.com

 The LightWalk

The LightWalk

LUMIÈRE
du Jour

Expérimenter la paix et le success au quotidien.

Lumière du Jour est votre dévotion quotidienne qui renouvelle votre esprit avec les pensées de Dieu concernant votre marche paisible dans la vie. Elle garantit le succès dans votre santé, vos relations, votre entreprise, votre carrière ou vos études.

+237 654 512 218

Lddsubscribe@gmail.com

The LightWalk

The LightWalk

SOWING TO THE SPIRIT

The Lord Jesus Christ in Luke 16:8 said, **"… for the children of this world are in their generation wiser than the children of light."** Then the wise speaking along this same line of thought in Ecclesiastes 10:5-7 says, **"There is an evil which I have seen under the sun, as an error which proceedeth from the ruler: Folly is set in great dignity, and the rich sit in low place. I have seen servants upon horses, and princes walking as servants upon the earth"**.

What really is this error which has made the rich to sit in low places, kept princes living as servants, and has made servants to ride on horses? For many years in my Christian journey, I wondered how the children of the world could be wiser than the children of light; that must be an error indeed! Over the years, the Lord has taught me how to turn this table around, and maintain the dignity of His wisdom, as a prince. And that is what I am delighted to share with you in this book **"Sowing to the Spirit"**.

To order please contact:

Cameroon:

+237 243 858 491

+237 654 512 218

ALSO AVAILABLE ON
amazon.com

AURABOOKS
Read | Conceive | Write

NOTES

NOTES

9 798859 136276